INTREPID

WARRIORS

Living a Life of Fearless Intercession

Intrepid Warriors

Living a Life of Fearless Intercession

Tracee Anne Loosle

Published by XP Publishing
A department of XP Ministries
P.O. Box 1017, Maricopa, Arizona 85139
www.XPpublishing.com

ISBN-13: 978-1-62166087-3

Printed in the United States of America.
For worldwide distribution.

Dedication

I dedicate this book to my precious friend
and mentor, Mary Lawson. Because of Mary's
steadfast love and kindness toward me as she
taught me the ways of the Lord and how not to
agree with the enemy,

I am an Intrepid Warrior.

Contents

INCREDIO hope

www.intrepidheart.org/donate

Intrepid Hope is the compassion heart of Intrepid Heart Ministries and represents many hearts and hands in partnership, bringing HOPE and meeting the needs of adults and children. Intrepid Hope is impacting lives in Brazil, South Africa, Israel and other nations where the heart of God directs our steps.

"Now therefore, do not be afraid. I will provide for and support you and your little ones..."
Genesis 50:21

INTREPID HEART

Heal • Encourage • Awaken • Love

Tracee Anne Loosle is a woman full of God's love and contagious joy, releasing healing and awakening through the intercession of Jesus Christ. She is a transformation specialist ministering prophetically through the power of Holy Spirit, revealing the Father's heart. As a poet and author, her words strengthen, transform and encourage.

She is the founder and director of Intrepid Heart Ministries, an international ministry, and Intrepid Hope, the compassion arm of Intrepid Heart Ministries. She shares the joy of life with her husband Randy and their family.

• INTREPID HEART MINISTRIES •
P.O. Box 13847 Ogden, Utah 84412 | 801.782.5663 || www.intrepidheart.org

Foreword

I have known Tracee Loosle for over a decade. She is a woman after the heart of God. When I recommend a book, I do so because I know that the author is trustworthy and a person of integrity, living what they teach. Tracee is such a person. She lives what you will find in the pages of this book. Her life is characterized not only by integrity but also by grace and mercy.

Tracee's labor of love in prayer yields a strong intercessory hedge of protection around the ministry of Global Awakening. She leads intercession for our international ministry trips and for my prayer shield, which covers me and other key ministry leaders. She is a great blessing to our teams with her leadership, her teachings, and the powerful experiences that take place under her leadership. Her insights into intercession and breakthroughs in prayer are so exciting for our team members that they volunteer freely to pray during our conferences. During times of spiritual opposition, as the intercessory team experiences breakthrough we will experience the same breakthrough in our meetings. Often the team tells us that they were interceding just minutes before key points of breakthrough began to happen, or just before the direction I took in the meeting changed.

Tracee's new book, *Intrepid Warriors: Living a Life of Fearless Intercession*, will build your faith for intercession, clarifying concepts and beliefs that will enable you to enter new levels of breakthrough. This is a "how to" book and much more. *Intrepid Warriors* is the exciting story of the redemptive love and grace of Christ in and through Tracee's life. I believe this book will change your understanding of prayer and increase your faith for the possibilities of the power of prayer. I believe that through this book you will experience a greater intimacy with God. Tracee doesn't give us theory she has read in someone else's books, but rather she gives us what the Holy Spirit has taught her during her many hours of intercession and intimacy with the Lord. Now, through *Intrepid Warriors* you, too, have the opportunity to gain personal training from Tracee Anne Loosle and enter into new realms with God through prayer. I highly recommend Tracee to you, and I highly recommend *Intrepid Warriors*.

—Randy Clark
Founder and President of Global Awakening
and the Apostolic Network of Global Awakening

Acknowledgments

THANK YOU to my husband, Randy, who loves me like Christ loves His church. He has laid down his life so that together we can follow the path of the Intrepid Warrior.

Thank you, Randy Clark, for taking "lil ole me's" to the nations, training and releasing us to do what God calls us to do. Because of your faith and obedience to God, my life is one of God's adventure, power, love, grace, and glory.

Thank you, Susan Thompson, for your beautiful editing and making sense of my story and journey. There are many more miles to journey through your heart and gift.

Thank you to Intrepid Warrior Jennifer Michaelos who assisted in researching the scriptures for chapter 12 when she was my intern.

Thank you to Patricia King and the XP Ministries team. You are making history by stepping into the media realm. Thank you to the XP Publishing team, Lila Nelson, Steve Fryer, and Carol Martinez. Your creative collaboration has brought my dream to print.

Introduction

INTERCESSION IS A JOURNEY into the heart of the Father. Every adventure or assignment is unique and it is imperative to discern the Father's purpose. The lives of those we intercede for can literally depend on it. Sometimes we know God's purpose before we begin, sometimes as we go, and there are times when the knowing unfolds minute by minute. Intercession is truly an adventure and there is nothing more exciting than following the Lord into the great unknown.

My mission as an intercessor is to go where the Lord sends me. Sometimes when I'm going to other nations it feels like I'm stepping into an unknown galaxy. But the invitation from the Lord is to live a life that is without the boundaries of manmade religion; without fear, doubt, or unbelief. God is alive, and He is the same yesterday, today, and tomorrow. He is still healing, saving, and delivering nations.

My own great adventure with the Lord has happened in the most unexpected ways. It's been a journey, a pilgrimage, and often it's been a mystery; a continuously unfolding mystery written by the Author of creation. As each one of you embarks on the journey of discovering who you are in Christ, I believe that you, too, will engage in a mystery of epic proportions. You can become a part of God's great "Love Revolution," a renaissance of creative believers empowered with the Father's heart.

My story is uniquely mine, and the fruit of my encounters are the evidence that each glance, each touch, each time of filling changes us and empowers us. This is not intended to be a theological book, although it has sound teaching from the Word of God. Mostly it is a collection of my stories and insights that have opened the realm of heaven's possibilities, as I learn to partner with a God who still moves in mysterious and miraculous ways. I stand in awe of the Lord.

It is my hope and prayer that these stories and teachings will inspire you to pursue your own personal journey of discovery and encounters with our loving Father, whose heart of love is waiting to draw you into His presence.

Intrepid Heart

by Tracee Anne Loosle

Intrepid hearts are rising
from their slumber
Awakening in the dawn of the
bright morning star
Messengers of holy radical love
dispelling darkness
Ministers of blazing fire and
everlasting love
In His hands weapons fashioned
from praise
Songs of freedom releasing an
army of worshippers
Wooing His sons and daughters
awake and arise
His call reverberating
"do not be afraid"
Be strong and courageous in
God's mighty power
Be filled with Holy Spirit's
burning passion
Setting hearts aflame for the
love of Jesus
Sealed in the intrepid heart
of the Father

1

Revelatory Intercession

Begins

THE PERSON I AM TODAY is a far cry from the angry, hurt young woman I was before God got hold of me with His Holy Spirit. I had been a follower of Jesus for about eight years, but I was worn out. The unhealed places in my heart had me going around the same mountain over and over again. I had strongholds and wounds and a lot of generational iniquity operating in my life. I thought that in order to live a "successful Christian life" I had to wear a mask to hide what I was really feeling. In pain, ashamed, and confused, there were times when I locked myself in my room so that my negative emotions wouldn't spill over onto my family.

One day, lying in bed recovering from surgery, God shattered all of my paradigms and set me free. The Holy Spirit spoke to me and told me to get out of bed and turn on TBN.

Now understand, TBN is a cable channel and we didn't have cable at that time, but God's voice was unmistakable, so I got up and turned on the television. To my utter amazement TBN was on just as clear as could be, and Benny Hinn was ministering. At that point in my "walk" I was very opposed to what was going on with people like Benny Hinn because I had been told that this was not of God.

As the presence of the Lord filled my room, I found myself on my knees weeping as His holiness and weighty presence came upon me. I began to experience the Lord as I had never known Him before. He spoke to me and told me not to touch His anointed, that Benny Hinn was His man. And He began to open my eyes to see that His Spirit and His gifts are for today. Awash in His presence, I could feel the power of His grace and glory. Overcome by His Spirit, the words of Psalm 16:11 came to me: "You will make known to me the path of life; in Your presence is fullness of joy; in Your right hand there are pleasures forever."

From that moment on, I began to pursue God passionately. I was hungry and thirsty for the Word of God and for everything that the Word says is ours as a believer. I devoured

As the presence of the Lord filled my room, I found myself on my knees weeping as His holiness and weighty presence came upon me. I began to experience the Lord as I had never known Him before.

the Word like a starving person. I fasted and prayed, seeking God with all my heart. I wanted everything He had to offer. I couldn't wait to discover what it meant to live in the fullness of Christ and His healing grace. I didn't realize it at the time, but this was the beginning of an intense period of spiritual formation that would change me from a confused young woman into a fearless, intrepid warrior.

Suddenly, I was eager to go where God was moving in power so that I could experience that power more fully in my life. I tried to get to the Brownsville Revival in Florida and the Toronto Blessing in Canada but found myself instead at a conference in Hampton, Virginia. The year was 1997. John and Brenda Kilpatrick were the keynote speakers. Prior to the conference, God instructed me to do a twenty-one day "Daniel" fast – a body, soul, and spirit preparation. As the fast progressed, I found myself moving into a place of deep intimacy with the Lord.

The Sunday before the conference, I went with my friend Cheryl to the morning service at her church, where the conference was being held. During worship I was healed of a hip-flexor joint injury that had plagued me for quite a long time. I was able to dance before the Lord, pain free!

The pastor's message that morning included stories of what God was doing in the world. One story in particular puzzled and intrigued me. It was of a minister in England who was experiencing signs of supernatural oil in his hands with the evidence of healing anointing. His story increased my faith and my hunger for more of God.

The message for the evening service was all about the fire of God on the altar of our lives and how it never goes out. When the altar call came. I rushed forward, crying out to God for His fire. After a time of crying out, I noticed that I had oil on the tips of my hair. I quizzed my friend Cheryl to see if anyone had anointed my hair, but no one had. God had touched me!

As the conference began the next night, the atmosphere was charged with the electric power of faith and hope, and I was very expectant. John Kilpatrick, the pastor of Brownsville Assembly of God, where revival was still happening, was the speaker that night. His message was powerful and it began to release faith in me. I had no idea what I was expecting but my heart was ready – ready for God to do something.

I longed to be an overcomer, no longer afraid. I wanted to live with the power and might that God said was available to those who believed in Him. As John Kilpatrick began to go through the congregation praying for people, he came to me, stopped, waved his handkerchief, and prayed a simple prayer. For the next hour and a half, I was in God's presence. At times He would pin me to the floor and at other times I rolled and rolled around the room.

My friend Cheryl and another woman brought people to pray for me. I began to experience pain as the intense presence and power of God removed things from my soul. As each thing was removed, I could feel God's life and love come

From that point on, I had a burning passion for intercession. I found that I had to pray and spend time with the Lord. I lived and breathed in His life. As I began to intercede, I saw God move in so many ways.

into me. I was undone. Words can never describe what happened to me. When I got up off the floor, I was not the same. I had been baptized in the Holy Spirit and fire!

Cheryl and I tried to talk about what had happened, but I couldn't describe it. All I knew was that now I had the enabling power of God's Spirit at work in me. On the flight home, God told me that I would no longer be under the influence of the powers and principalities in the region where I lived, that I would never be oppressed or depressed again in that land or anywhere else. When I arrived at the airport, my husband was waiting and he noticed a difference in me, too. I couldn't explain to him what had happened except to say that I had encountered God and He had changed me.

From that point on, I had a burning passion for intercession. I found that I *had* to pray and spend time with the Lord. I lived and breathed in *His* life. As I began to intercede, I saw God move in so many ways. Prayers were answered quickly, discernment was clearer, love was greater, and vision increased. I was being set free and healed! Life became more purposeful. It was a new beginning for me.

And then the assignments began to come in. It was as if Holy Spirit whispered to me, "This is your mission should you choose to accept it." Each small step of obedience unveiled the mystery, the adventure, and the destiny God had for me. I found myself accepting assignments and following the Lord from a place of greater dependence on Him, living life in the power of His Holy Spirit.

2

International Mission Intercession

He will cover you with his feathers, and under his wings you will find refuge; his faithfulness will be your shield and rampart.　　　　　　　　—Psalm 91:4 NIV

GOD CHANGES US FROM THE INSIDE OUT. Before I was baptized in the Holy Spirit, I had been a critic of people such as Randy Clark and the mighty move of the Spirit that was taking place in Toronto, Canada. I believed the enemy's lies that the gifts of the Holy Spirit are not for today. As God renewed and transformed my mind and I became hungry for all that He had for me, I found old lies falling away. I was of a different spirit now; expectant, hungry for more of God, and filled with a believing faith that, truly, with God all things are possible.

During this time the Lord called me to a conference in Salt Lake City, and I found myself an intercessor on the wall for Randy Clark. The presence of God was tangible at the conference; the atmosphere was electric with His power and love. During the video presentation of Global Awakening's international mission trips, I felt the Lord's prompting on my heart to go! Global Awakening's mission work in Brazil caught my attention, and I began to set my heart on Brazil, not realizing that I was no longer the one who decided such things.

God lovingly began to teach me about obedience. He closed the door on Brazil and opened the door to the Ukraine. Not long after, twelve of us from my church in Utah found ourselves on a flight bound for Kiev, Ukraine. That would be our first stop; then we would travel to Odessa and Nikolayev. Compelled by the love of God to go where I had never been before, I, who had once dreamed of traveling for adventure, found myself traveling for the Lord and for *His* purposes.

The anticipation of what God would do increased as we checked into our flight, and it continued to build as we waited for a red eye to take us through Germany en route to Kiev, Ukraine. We were set apart and filled with wide-eyed wonder, yet I was battling fear. It was a fear of the unknown and of going without my husband to a foreign land. Sitting in my chair at the gate waiting for our boarding announcement, I prayed silently to God, pleading for Him to help me. At that moment, a white feather floated down and fell into my lap and I heard Holy Spirit speak to me from Psalm 91:

Under the guidance of the Holy Spirit, the direction for our intercession emerged. We were to wait upon the Lord and to watch and see what He was doing.

He will cover you with his feathers, and under his wings you will find refuge. —Psalm 91:4 NIV

I was flooded with peace and I knew without a doubt that God would protect me and be with me. This was only the beginning of the signs and wonders of God. I was soon challenged in every realm as I experienced the Kingdom of God in power. Every limitation was shattered as I jumped fully into all that Jesus had for me.

When we arrived in the Ukraine, we had orientation with Tom Rutoluo, Randy Clark's right-hand man at the time and director of international ministry trips for Global Awakening. At one point, Tom explained how the team had intercession going on during the meetings and the night watches, and asked for a volunteer to lead. I was hesitant and unsure and didn't volunteer, but neither did anyone else.

That night the Holy Spirit began to deal with me on this issue, and in the morning I agreed to lead. Tom interviewed me and the baton was passed. I had accepted my first intercession mission on an international ministry team! I knew I was about to join God on a special assignment.

Under the guidance of the Holy Spirit, the direction for our intercession emerged. We were to wait upon the Lord and to watch and see what He was doing. God released revelation as we spent time worshipping Him and giving Him glory and honor. Some heard His voice, others felt His direction and some had visions. There were times when we could smell the fragrance of the Lord.

As He showed us things in prayer and we came into agreement with Him, He began to do those things in the services. Most of us had never encountered the Lord in these ways. Up until that time I had only heard stories of such things, but I was now experiencing them myself. What joy!

One night in Odessa, we stopped to pray for a young boy named Vladik who was about ten years old and deaf in one ear. I asked Lena, my interpreter, to pray with us and interpret. As I began to pray, my hand became very hot and as red as the sweater I was wearing. Vladik's ear also became hot and bright red. The presence of God was powerful. His holy fire was all over us as I asked God to recreate Vladik's ear. He was touched by the Holy Spirit and fell out in the Spirit.

Vladik told us later that at the moment he was touched by the Holy Spirit he felt wind come into him. When he was able, his mother had him cover his good ear and she spoke very quietly into the ear that was deaf. He was able to repeat everything she said. Another interpreter confirmed the miracle! I started weeping and jumping up and down, praising God for this healing. Vladik and his mother shared their testimony, as God received all the glory.

When Randy heard of this healing, he asked Vladik, his mother, and me to pray for a young woman who only had fifty percent of her hearing. We prayed briefly before the service, instructing her to enter into worship and telling her we would pray for her after the message. When she came to us after the message, Vladik felt the wind of God come into him and he told her not to be afraid. Touched by the power of God, she fell in His presence and was filled with peace as the Lord moved over her in gentle waves of healing love. We had her close her eyes as the interpreter whispered to her. She heard his whisper! She was beautifully healed by the Lord. After that, Vladik was my prayer partner for the remainder of the evening and the next, and together we saw the Lord heal many people.

The Lion and the Lamb

During intercession on the second night in Odessa, we experienced an amazing visitation. My team and I started out the evening leading a fire tunnel. After the fire tunnel, the pastors of the Messianic congregation asked us to pray for them. While we were preparing to pray, Steve, one of our team members, began to travail in deep intercession as he realized that we were in the hall he had dreamt about the night before. I, too, felt led to pray to the Lord for His revelation so that we could intercede for His purposes to come forth.

As we began to pray, the Lord touched the pastors and spoke words of life to them through our team. They fell to the floor under the power of Holy Spirit and soon I ended up on the floor, too, drawn into the prophetic experience that was unfolding. As I began to experience the glory of the Lord, I saw the golden mane of a lion with the face of a lamb. The Holy Spirit moved in me and I began to prophesy, "He's the Lion and the Lamb." I said this over and over again and then I began to declare, "He's the Lion from the tribe of Judah." Those around me said that my upper body would rise up and my right hand would point, declaring for the people to receive Him, the Lion and the Lamb. Then I began to speak in tongues and battle with my hands calling the lost into the Kingdom. As I did this I saw a golden, pink light as the heavens opened releasing the favor of God.

With access to the heavenly realm open, I prayed for revival. It was an intense and very real encounter with the Lord. I still see His eyes of holy fire both tender and fierce. The remainder of the night was marked by miracles and healings. When we arrived in Nikolayev the next night and I was in intercession, Linda came and took me into the auditorium where the meetings were being held. Over the platform was a very large banner of the Lion and the Lamb. At the top of the banner were the words, "He's the Lion and the Lamb,"

With access to the heavenly realm open, I prayed for revival. It was an intense and very real encounter with the Lord. I still see His eyes of holy fire both tender and fierce. The remainder of the night was marked by miracles and healings.

and at the bottom were the words, "He's the Lion from the tribe of Judah."

In Nikolayev I began to understand what the Lord was saying about the Lion and the Lamb. We saw the Lion roar in the face of the enemy and we saw the gentle healing of the Lamb. We heard His prophetic voice calling His people to the Kingdom. Many lives were healed and saved and delivered during our time in the Ukraine. The people we ministered to will never be the same and neither will we.

I had seen feathers and had them appear on my clothing; feathers not like anything here on earth. There were signs everywhere that God was keeping us hidden under the shadow of His wings. We knew He had angels watching over us everywhere we went. After that trip, I knew that the safest place to be is in the will of God.

The nations were written into my heart on my first trip to the Ukraine. I experienced not just the tenderness of His love but also the fierceness of His love that calls us into battle so that all may know Him. With God all things are possible!

3

When We Intercede

TO INTERCEDE IS NOT JUST TO PRAY, but to partner with God that His Kingdom come and His will be done on earth as it is in heaven. As we intercede in obedience, God opens doors through His Son Jesus. Jesus is the door. Access to the Father's Kingdom comes through Him and Him alone. The Holy Spirit is here to partner with us, empowering us to live in Christ and to minister in His name, bringing His light into the darkness.

In 2000, the Lord pulled me aside from corporate intercessory gatherings and spoke to me very clearly that for a season I was not to read any more books on intercession. He wanted to be my teacher. One of the first things He showed me during this season of learning was that most prayer gatherings were not as effective as they could be because we are not in unity with what God is doing. Many of our prayer gatherings are filled with individuals with their own agendas. In this kind of setting, our prayers become more self-focused on what is affecting our own lives, instead of being focused on what God is trying to do through us. It is as if we have our own little guns and we're shooting them off in all different directions.

It is important for us to remember that we are not called into corporate prayer to be lone shooters, but to come together in the bonds of peace and in unity of spirit as one and for God. While there is a time and a place to gather to pray for one another's needs, when we come together in corporate intercession to pray for one specific purpose, such as for a church, or a business, or a school, or the government, or whatever it might be, we need to focus on what the Father's heart is for that situation. God desires that corporate prayer be focused on the revelation that we receive from Him.

When we are able to focus our prayers on God's revelation for the situation, we become a guided missile that goes directly for *His* target. When we wait upon Him we will hear what He is saying and our prayers will hit their mark. From our place of waiting we learn to discern His voice – that place of intimate friendship and fellowship with the Lord. In this place of focused prayer, heaven comes down and invades the earth with the strategies and blueprints and the heart of the Father. There is no other way. Too many times the prayers we pray are not in agreement with the Kingdom of light and, therefore, not God ordained. Who and what we agree with is who and what we empower.

Corporate intercession is a treasure hunt and we need to understand that God holds the *keys*. As we seek His face through times of intimate worship and prayer, waiting on Him, He will open our eyes to see a *key* on the map. He will open our ears to hear His voice saying, "This is the way to go." He will unlock our hearts to know His plans. Those who seek God and His will are able to be the successful partners that God desires.

As intercessors, when we pray we are fighting for the causes of heaven. We are seeing into a situation with the holy eyes of God's justice. The enemy releases many lies to trick and ensnare us, so as to cause gaps and breaches between God and His people. Our role in intercession is to fight for the justice of heaven.

> I looked for someone among them who would build up the wall and stand before me in the gap on behalf of the land so I would not have to destroy it, but I found no one. —Ezekiel 22:30 NIV

God is looking for those who will build up a wall of defense around His Kingdom people. He is looking for those

Corporate intercession is a treasure hunt and we need to understand that God holds the keys. As we seek His face through times of intimate worship and prayer, waiting on Him, He will open our eyes to see a key on the map.

who will present themselves to be the ones who arise with the strategy of the Lord, who endure and persevere without running from the battle, who become servant intercessors. It is from this position, as we stand in the gap, that the gap is healed. We operate from a position of trust in God.

David was a shepherd who tended his father's sheep, defending them from predators. He learned to kill the enemy in the wilderness while watching over someone else's sheep. When his father called him from the fields to take provisions to his brothers, he had no idea he was about to be catapulted into a great battle; yet, he was prepared. He knew how to trust God, and that was his greatest strength. He knew how to move in agreement with God.

Beloved, if God the Father gives us a prayer to pray, then we can be sure that prayer has already been answered! This is the powerful prayer of agreement; as intercessors, it is important for us to understand what is meant by the prayer of agreement. When we agree with what the Lord is doing and saying, He moves. He can do anything without us, but He chooses to partner with us.

Servant Towel Intercessors

As I sit under God's tutelage, learning to be one of His intercessors, one of the things that He has placed strongly on my heart is the breach between leaders and intercessors. As I wrestled in prayer with this issue, God gave me a revelation about intercessors as servants. This revelation has never left me, even though it came to me years ago. It is a simple vision of intercessors who humble themselves and receive from the Lord the servant's apron and towel of intercession. Equipped with these things, we are able to serve those we are called to stand alongside. We are to be impeccable in our service to the ones God has called us to.

The setting in this vision is like a formal state dinner at the White House. The guests are VIPs. The intercessors do not take off the servant aprons but go about their duties with steadfast devotion. The VIPs do not even notice the intercessors are there, but everything they need is given to them before they even realize they need it. Through this vision, the Lord revealed to me that many of us who feel we are called to intercession want the place of the VIP rather than seeing the necessity of our role as servants. As intercessors we are to serve the ones the Lord sends us, without any expectations.

I know from personal experience that this kind of servant intercession can be a challenge. Many intercessors are also leaders. But as leaders, it is very important that we understand that we are called by Christ to serve with a humble heart of love. Jesus is our model. Just as He washed His disciple's feet, we also should be able to wash one another's feet with the heart of a servant. This is a place of humility. The Lord loves a humble heart, yet He knows how our human hearts can struggle to make a place for humility to take up residence.

When I had the vision of putting on the servant towel of intercession, I was personally convicted of the many times

I had wanted someone to recognize the hours I'd spent in prayer on their behalf. Since that time I have had many reminders from the Lord about going to this place of humility. There are those times when others are promoted or receive special recognition for things they have done, and I may be passed by. But oh, the place of grace and humility to stay hidden in Christ and not need the approval of man, to live instead for the approval of the One! Jesus came as a humble man, not seeking approval or recognition. He lived a life of confidence in His Father's will. As we seek to pray and be like Jesus, walking with a servant's heart as intercessors in His footsteps, we will find the greatest reward – His blessings and His presence.

One of my servant towel intercession testimonies came about when I thought I was invited in as the "specialist" to lead intercession at an event. I was surprised to find out that not only was I not the specialist, but I was actually stepping on someone else's toes, invading the place God had for them. As I sought the Lord about what was happening, He revealed that there was a misunderstanding. He instructed me to submit to the one He had placed in charge, even though I had been led to believe it was me. Submitting to the Lord as He had directed me, I apologized for any way I may have overstepped my place.

Reminding me of His model of servant intercession, He took me back to a prophetic painting I had done of the seven mountains, which came by revelation. In this painting, a keyhole appeared at the bottom. Now, I did not draw or paint

Let us make no mistake: the enemy would like to draw us into a position of pride because he knows God resists the proud but gives grace to the humble. We are sons and daughters first, but we cannot forget that love also serves.

the keyhole; it simply appeared there at the bottom of the mountains that I had painted. The Lord began to remind me that the only way up His mountain is to humble ourselves and go through the low keyhole at the base of mountain.

As I began to understand this revelation, He told me that if I would walk in love and honor, with a servant's heart, stepping back from the prominent place, He would turn things around. It was not easy and I had to ask Him for help, but as I embraced the process of humility, the Lord moved in everyone's heart. The one who was leading was able to grow in their gifting, and as they were honored they soared in the love and acceptance that God was pouring out on them. God turned everything around and the enemy did not win. Humility brought the situation to a place of triumph.

We must understand that pride is a very dangerous place. Let us make no mistake: the enemy would like to draw us into a position of pride because he knows God resists the proud but gives grace to the humble. We are sons and daughters first, but we cannot forget that love also serves. Has the enemy ever taken you out of your place because you sought position? We need to be in our place. God is constantly aligning us for our assignments. Everyone has a place. Let God reveal your place to you through the open windows of heaven. When we stand in our place of humility, next to the heart of Christ, we can effectively partner with God.

Jesus constantly modeled this place of humble service to us when He lived as a man on this earth. When a woman caught in adultery was thrown at His feet, He simply knelt and wrote in the sand. Only those present and those in heaven know what was written that day. He did not condemn her in her sin but instead silenced the voice of her accusers. His love healed the place the enemy had used to break into her life. This is a picture of holy advocacy, of servant intercession. Jesus' love, His compassion, and His words set her free. He is still making intercession for us today.

> Therefore he is able to save completely those who come to God through him, because he always lives to intercede for them. —Hebrews 7:25 NIV

As sons and daughters who are His friends, we can serve like He did.

Lord, help us to see the opportunity to serve through our intercession. Amen.

4

Spiritually Aligned

Intercession

A LIGNMENT IS A KEY to moving in prophetic and revelatory intercession. As intercessors, our first alignment is to God. We must be spiritually aligned with the Kingdom of heaven so that we can become mighty weapons in the hand of the Father. We want to be aligned with His Word because it keeps us pure in heart and thought.

Being aligned in honor to God brings alignment in our households, with our leaders, to our government, and within the body of Christ, the church. When we are aligned with a heart of honor, honor will position us with the Father. Honor is having respect for others and treating them according to their place in the Kingdom. All people should be honored. Honor is a heart attitude that will align us with the Father's heart. And most importantly, as intercessors we must seek the alignment of love so that the compassionate heart of God can move us to travail in prayer for those in need.

Alignment in Humility

In order to come into a place of spiritually aligned intercession, we must first align ourselves in humility to God. If we want the glory of the Lord to come into our meetings, the places we go, the places of prayer and intercession, we need to be humble. God resists the proud. To humble ourselves, we must get into a place of submitting to God's lordship in our life without resisting His direction and correction. When we do this, His love will lift us up. God will help us to walk in humility and love in every situation we encounter when we submit to Him. Humility is vital to a life of fearless intercession. James tells us that God resists the proud but gives grace to the humble.

> All of you, clothe yourselves with humility toward one another, because "God opposes the proud but shows favor to the humble." —1 Peter 5:5 NIV

> Be completely humble and gentle; be patient, bearing with one another in love. —Ephesians 4:2 NIV

When we come into that place of humility before God, we preserve the unity of the Spirit. We become part of that one body, that one hope, that "one Lord, one faith, one baptism; one God and Father of all, who is over all and through all and in all" (Ephesians 4:5-6 NIV). In so doing, we can begin:

Speaking the truth in love, we will grow to become in every respect the mature body of him who is the head, that is, Christ. From him the whole body, joined and held together by every supporting ligament, grows and builds itself up in love, as each part does its work.

—Ephesians 4:15-16 NIV

We should never look to be exalted. The Lord brought this home to me in a very painful way. At that time I was over the ministries of both intercession and the prophetic at our church. I was in a position of authority and the enemy came to dislodge me, trying to use flattery to pull me into a place of sin, and he almost succeeded. To destroy my life and the life of the church, the enemy found a wound in me, a place where he could put his hook. He took an old wound and opened it up, putting up offenses between me and the leadership of the church. Things began to fall apart. Unkind words were said and I was deeply hurt. As I sought the Lord, He brought me to Proverbs:

The fear of the Lord is the instruction for wisdom, and before honor comes humility.   —Proverbs 15:33

The Lord showed me that this wound had me looking for honor and validation. I was undone! The breach with the leadership of the church was repaired as I repented and came into a place of humble service. The enemy didn't succeed in destroying me or the ministries of intercession and the prophetic in our church.

Humility always gives God the glory. Our best example of humility is found in Jesus. He invites us to take His yoke upon us and learn from Him how to be gentle and humble in heart. When we do, we will find rest for our souls. As we put on Christ, we put on His heart of compassion, of kindness, of humility, of gentleness, and of patience. It is from this position we are able to put on His love. And His love is the perfect bond of unity.

In the gospel of Luke, chapter 22, we see Jesus trying to explain to His disciples that humility is the foremost test of a truly great person or leader. He tells them not to look at the model of the world to understand leadership, but to understand what leadership means in the Kingdom of God. In the Kingdom of God, the one called to lead must not be the one sitting at the table but the one who serves those sitting at the table. In order to lead, we must first understand what it means to serve.

Alignment to the Word of God

When we come into intercession, the Word is our powerful tool. It is our sword, the sword of the Spirit. We need to have alignment with the Word of God. We need to know the Word and be in the Word so that it can be released in prayer. God's Word is very powerful and it will not return void, but will go out and accomplish what He sends it to do. I love God's Word. It protects us and it keeps us pure.

> How can a young man keep his way pure? By keeping it according to Your word.　　　　　—Psalm 119:9

When we come into intercession, the Word is our powerful
tool. It is our sword, the sword of the Spirit. We need
to know the Word and be in the Word so that it can be
released in prayer.

When Jesus began His earthly ministry, He demonstrated
to us the importance and the power of the Word of God in
the life of every believer. After His baptism, Jesus was led by
the Spirit into the wilderness for forty days and was tempted
by the devil. He fasted during this time, and we're told that
He became hungry. When the devil came to Him and tempted Him to turn stones into bread, Jesus answered him and
said,

> It is written, 'Man shall not live on bread alone, but
> on every word that proceeds out of the mouth of
> God.'   —Matthew 4:11

When we become spiritually hungry and need sustenance,
we should feast on the Word of God. God's Word comes
directly from His mouth and it is life to our spirits. As intercessors, we should feast continuously on the Word of God,
coming to His lavishly set banquet table many times a day.

When we treasure God's Word in our hearts, we won't
sin against Him. When we take delight in His statutes, we
won't forget them. When we put on the mind of Christ

and become hidden in Christ, submitting to His lordship through His Word, we can be used effectively as intercessors. Alignment to the Word brings our thoughts into line with the mind of Christ so that when thoughts come that aren't pure or lovely or worthy of praise, we will stop and question where they are coming from. If we hold them up to the light of Scripture and find they aren't aligning, we need to take them captive to Christ.

> For though we live in the world, we do not wage war as the world does. The weapons we fight with are not the weapons of the world. On the contrary, they have divine power to demolish strongholds. We demolish arguments and every pretension that sets itself up against the knowledge of God, and we take captive every thought to make it obedient to Christ. And we will be ready to punish every act of disobedience, once your obedience is complete.
>
> —2 Corinthians 10:3-6 NIV

When we take those thoughts captive, we are asking the Spirit of the Lord to go in and remove them, replacing them with what is worthy.

> Finally brethren, whatever is true, whatever is honorable, whatever is right, whatever is pure, whatever is lovely, whatever is of good repute, if there is any excellence and if anything worthy of praise, dwell on these things.   —Philippians 4:8

Alignment in All Areas of Our Life

I believe we need to be aligned with Christ in every area of our lives – in our homes, to the leadership of our church, to our government leaders, in the body of Christ, and in love. I have seen too many people come into intercession who are so wounded they don't want to submit anywhere. Instead of bringing power to the team, they bring disunity. There have been times when I am leading intercession that I have had to literally shut the door and only allow those I had invited in to pray. I don't like to do that, but for the sake of God's purposes I cannot have someone come in and bring disunity.

Alignment in Our Household

I believe strongly that we need to be aligned in our households, submitted as husbands and wives one to another. There has been much said about this message from Scripture, and it is not my intent to debate it here, but I have seen the fruit of it in my own life. We are never to submit to abuse, but when we submit to one another in love, we come into alignment with God's Word. What God has done in our household is wonderful. The glory of the Lord is coming and filling our house.

Alignment to Church Leadership

I also believe strongly that we need to be submitted to our leaders in the church, to be aligned with them. The Lord literally breathed this Scripture on me:

> Have confidence in your leaders and submit to their authority, because they keep watch over you as those who must give an account. Do this so that their work will be a joy, not a burden, for that would be of no benefit to you.　　　　　　—Hebrews 13:17 NIV

Again, I am not advocating that we submit to abuse. Sadly, there has been too much abuse in the church. If you are in a place that is not healthy, I urge you to seek the Lord and ask Him to put you in a healthy church. It is never God's intent for you to be abused. Instead, His Word tells us to submit to godly leadership in the church.

Alignment to Government Leadership

It's very important to understand what it means to submit to those in leadership in our government. We may disagree with what they are doing, but when that happens we need to get with God and ask Him how we can pray for them. We should not go around badmouthing our leaders. When we honor them, we shut up the foolish acts of men.

> Submit yourselves for the Lord's sake to every human authority: whether to the emperor, as the supreme authority, or to governors, who are sent by him to punish those who do wrong and to commend those who do right.　　　　　　—1 Peter 2:13-14 NIV

We should not go around badmouthing our leaders. When we honor them, we shut up the foolish acts of men.

Alignment in the Body of Christ

It is vital that we understand the importance of alignment in the body of Christ, the church. Many of you have read C.S. Lewis' *Screwtape Letters* in which he brilliantly illustrates how the enemy has succeeded to such a great degree in sowing disunity in the body of Christ. It is time for the the body to come into unity, and I believe we are. I see such a difference in this season. I see *love* happening in the church. I see different streams and different expressions of God finding acceptance. The world will notice when the church comes into unity.

> For even as the body is one and yet has many members, and all the members of the body, though they are many, are one body, so also is Christ. For by one Spirit we were all baptized into one body, whether Jews or Greeks, whether slaves or free, and we were all made to drink of one Spirit.
>
> —1 Corinthians 12:12-13

Alignment in Love

Isn't it the love of God, the compassionate heart of God, that moves us to go pray for someone? Isn't it the love of God that takes us into hours of intercession for those who do not know the Lord? Isn't it the love of God that has us go to other nations where we don't have the comforts of home? If you are not motivated by the love of God, there may be works behind your actions rather than love. Go to God and ask Him to change your heart. Cry out for a baptism of love that submerges you in the depths of His love, taking you into the width, breadth, length, and height of His heart, into the fullness of His everlasting love.

On another occasion I was on a mission trip in India. One night in a service, as I was kneeling in prayer and interceding for our leaders, I looked up and saw the faces of all the people waiting to receive a touch from God and be healed; I was undone. At that moment, God's love came in and broke my heart for India. Up until that point, I thought I had given my heart completely to the Lord. But this was different. I was utterly shattered and I knew that from then on, with God's help, no matter where He sent me, I would be able to stand in the gap for the people He put in front of me. Something had shifted in my heart.

When we pray from that deep place, our intercession comes from the place of *His* deep love, and His love overcomes all the evil that is present. As we allow the great carpenter of the universe, Jesus Christ, to apply His level to our lives, He will bring *His* alignment, lining us up with Him in love as He communicates spirit-to-spirit, speaking *to* us, *in* us, and *through* us, so that our intercession becomes prophetic and revelatory.

5

Power Keys

THROUGH HIS SPIRIT OF REVELATION the Lord has given me what I call "power keys" for intercessors and for every believer. These keys are meant to keep us going, pursuing the *"more, Lord"* that Randy Clark speaks about. Sometimes circumstances try to get us out of alignment with the will of God. The enemy will twist whatever he can and use it to his advantage to get us to focus on the problem instead of our "power source" (God) who solves all problems. But God gives us power keys to persevere.

Power to Persevere

We know we are to persevere in prayer, but prayer takes perseverance! Our prayer life can be likened to an oil lamp. An oil lamp needs to be filled with oil in order to give forth light. The wick has to be trimmed and at times replaced. The glass lampshade needs special cleaning so the light can shine through it. All this is preparation for the lamp to burn brightly. Likewise, as intercessors we need to constantly be filled up with the "oil" of the Holy Spirit. We need to keep our wicks trimmed by going before the Lord to be pruned of anything that is hindering our prayer life. And we can clean our glass lampshades as we worship, so that our light shines brightly to the world around us.

God exhorts us through His Word to persevere as we intercede. In the parable of the seed in the gospel of Luke, we see that preparation was needed for the soil to be ready to receive the seed. Likewise, it takes perseverance in our times of preparation with the Lord for the seed of God's revelation to take root. It needs to be nurtured and cultivated before we see its fruit.

Those who persevere with God are able to stand firm, fully clothed in His armor, ready for anything. We need to stand firm for those times when our circumstances and those we pray for are in opposition to God's promises. If we fail to spend time with the Lord, discovering His heart in the process of prayer, we may misread His purposes, causing us to judge or criticize the very process He walks us through to get to the answer.

I want to share some thoughts the Lord has given me on how to persevere in prayer and intercession with Him, because I believe they will help keep us on the path that leads to more of Him in our lives.

Obedience that Opens Doors

Staying on course with God as we intercede requires obedience.

> If anyone turns a deaf ear to my instruction, even their
> prayers are detestable.   —Proverbs 28:9 NIV

The Lord loves to answer the prayers of those who obey His voice. When I see the fulfillment of prophetic words and astounding answers to prayer, I believe it's because of obedience. I know it's not always easy to follow and obey. Sometimes, misunderstandings arise when we are challenged by God to obey Him in a way that doesn't make sense to us. However, I believe the rewards of obedience are worth any price we have to pay.

As God led the Israelites out of bondage into the Promised Land, He told them He would provide for them if they chose to obey Him and put Him first. He promised them a land far superior to Egypt that would be watered by rains from heaven and flowing with milk and honey. These were the rewards that would flow out of their obedience to the Lord. But when we ask, we must obey the answer that comes. When we seek, we must follow where He leads. When we

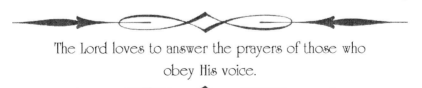

The Lord loves to answer the prayers of those who
obey His voice.

knock, we must walk through the door He opens. Obedience opens doors, allowing blessings to flow. It was hard for the Israelites, when they were in the desert, to understand the importance of obedience; it can be hard for us, too. Jesus tells us to seek first the Kingdom of God and all these things will be added unto us.

> But seek first his kingdom and his righteousness, and
> all these things will be given to you as well.
> —Matthew 6:33 NIV

Decrees that Dismantle

As true intercessors who care about what happens to those we stand in the gap for, we must get to that place in our lives where we know that our voice is being used, so that the voice of the Lord can be released in power. We become the trumpets, the instruments through which He can decree *His* decrees.

Many of us do not understand that the power in the decree comes from the humbled, obedient, and laid-down life of a lover who wants to please their King. Some speak decrees like they are grocery lists just waiting to be filled, because it is what they desire. Beloved, the only decrees we should speak are the ones that come straight from the heart of the Father. *His* decrees dismantle the schemes of the enemy.

We can learn a lot from Esther. She understood what it meant to be a laid-down lover who wants only to please the king. She was one who embraced the preparation process so that she might be pleasing and find favor with the king. She was intent on capturing his heart during her season of preparation. When faced with the schemes of the enemy, and with rejection and possible death, she approached the king from a prepared place. With fasting and prayer, she set a banquet for the king and her enemy, and God was with her. Her enemy was hung on the very gallows designed for her uncle, Mordecai, who was then placed in a position of great authority. The decree Mordecai released, with the seal of the king on it, dismantled all the plans and the actual decrees of the enemy. Because Esther was willing to become that laid-down lover, the enemy was defeated through her obedience.

Blessings that Build

We must strive to grasp the power of the blessing in intercession. So often Christians focus on the curses and the cause and effects, forgetting the power in the blessing. The blessing of God is all-powerful because it was purchased for us through the blood of Jesus Christ. He suffered, died, and rose again that we may now live on this earth in the abundant life, filled with all His fullness through His grace. Living from a place of His fullness and grace will cause us to release the fullness of the blessed life to others.

As intercessors, let us be the ones who choose to bless. Our prayers can be those that release life and blessings. Our actions can be to bless those the Lord sends us to if we take the time to hear the Father's heart for the ones we pray for. There really is life and death in the power of our words.

Through the blessing of the upright a city is exalted,
but by the mouth of the wicked it is destroyed.

—Proverbs 11:11 NIV

As intercessors and advocates and brokers of heaven, let us choose life. We should overflow with life! As we allow the living rivers of life from Christ within us to flow out of us, He will saturate every place, every person, and every assignment with His presence, causing the dry places to spring forth with His life and promise. Beauty will appear and glory will shine forth. Faith, hope, and love will remain and abide.

Sounds that Shift—Praise that Breaks Shackles

As intercessors we must be careful not to allow any schemes of the enemy to shackle us to darkness, remembering that praise breaks the shackles. Break off the shackles in your own life and help others to do the same. Do not allow rejection in one place to hold you back. Break off the shackles of rejection, criticism, betrayal, and negative words. Live free!

When we live a life of exuberant praise in every situation, no prison of man or the enemy can hold us. As we give thanks, the gates of heaven open, releasing that wonder-working power of God to deliver us. When Paul and Silas were beaten and thrown in prison, they began to pray and sing hymns of praise to God. Suddenly a great earthquake shook the prison, causing the doors to open and the chains to fall from the prisoners. At that moment every shackle in the prison was broken, and guards and prisoners alike were set free (Acts 16:22-26).

As we allow the living rivers of life from Christ within us to flow out of us, He will saturate every place, every person, and every assignment with His presence, causing the dry places to spring forth with His life and promise.

When we praise God as we intercede, the sounds of our praises release the mighty right hand of God. As an intercessor, let the sound of praise in you be released. Praise and worship are powerful weapons of warfare, causing us to enter into the courts of the Lord where we find fullness of joy in His presence.

I learned firsthand the power of praise in a conference in Brazil. The glory of the Lord was present as we interceded and began to minister to the people. As I began to pray for a man who was tall and quite strong, the power of God came on him and he flew up in the air. When he came down, the heel of his shoe landed directly on my foot, splitting open the top of my foot. The pain was intense, but I was on assignment with the Lord and in the midst of His glory. Crying out in the name of Jesus, I continued to minister.

I think I prayed for a dozen more people and then the Lord had me begin to read a poem, releasing it prophetically into the atmosphere of the room. As He did, we went into another realm of glory where He touched our hearts with His heart, drawing us deeper into Him. From this place of glory we continued to minister. By this time my foot was bleeding and I was starting to feel nauseous.

Some of the team members came over and began praying for my foot. One said he thought it might be broken. I was determined to stay in that place of praise and I started crying out, "Thank You, Lord, thank You that You are healing me." At that point we moved into the most powerful and glorious time of intercession.

God began to move and did many wonderful things in that meeting. By the time it was over, my foot was completely healed. Beloved, when we're in God's glory, miracles happen. Even in our weakest moments we can complete our assignments, because Christ's strength truly is made perfect in us!

6

Wrestling with Whom?

WE NEED TO UNDERSTAND who we are wrestling with when we find ourselves in that place of contending in prayer. Sometimes we are wrestling with the enemy and at other times it is the Lord. And it's also possible that we are wrestling with our own flesh and soul. When we seek the Lord and hear His voice, we can better understand whom we're wrestling with.

> After he had sent them across the stream, he sent over all his possessions. So Jacob was left alone, and a man wrestled with him till daybreak. When the man saw that he could not overpower him, he touched the socket of Jacob's hip so that his hip was wrenched as he wrestled with the man. Then the man said, "Let me go, for it is daybreak." But Jacob replied, "I will not let you go unless you bless me." The man asked him, "What is your name?" "Jacob," he answered.

Then the man said, "Your name will no longer be Jacob, but Israel, because you have struggled with God and with humans and have overcome."

—Genesis 32:23-28 NIV

When we find ourselves in a wrestling match with God, we might perceive that we need to convince the Lord of our position. But what may actually be happening is that God is changing positions and places in our heart and mind to come into alignment with who He says we are and what our destiny is.

When we join forces with others to intercede as a group, we may often find ourselves in a corporate wresting match. Tensions can emerge as each person struggles to embrace that prayerful wrestling position God has for them. We each have our own ideas and perceptions of what the prayer match should look like.

If our prayer strategies have been very effective in the past, and the fruit and the breakthroughs have been amazing, we have a tendency to think that we don't need to change our strategy. But we do! We need God's strategy, not our own. In a team-prayer event, God will empower us to win and see the victory when we lay aside our individual strategies and get His strategy. We have a heavenly coach who is directing the outcome, and all we need to do is yield to Him. If we boldly embrace the unknown, the Lord will show us a new way into the heart of a matter.

There is a corporate synergy of God's grace and power when we each fight the battle we are assigned to as a member of the team. There are many opponents that are about to be pinned and overcome as the body comes together. When the match seems hard, call on the name of the Lord – Jehovah-Nissi – the Lord, our Victorious Banner, who fights for us! As we partner with Him, He will change us into the ones who arise from the wrestling match with new names, new strengths, new resources, and the strategies of heaven! We will lay hold of the promises of God!

Wrestling in Love

I believe the greatest act of intercession is love. When we wrestle in prayer, we must wrestle with a heart of love. When we remember that the Father sent His only Son Jesus as *The Intercessor*, to give His life for all, we can begin to understand what that love really means. He took our place; He took our sins. Such amazing love was poured out for us!

> For God so loved the world, that He gave His only begotten Son, that whoever believes in Him shall not perish, but have eternal life. —John 3:16

The greatest joy we have in this life is to choose to love Him now with the way we live, the way we love, and the way we heal the breaches. To care about the world and the ones who are bound in darkness is to care about what touches the heart of the Father. As His beloved dear children, I believe it pleases His heart greatly to see us seeking and rescuing the lost with a heart of love, leaving behind judgment and condemnation.

> Therefore, there is now no condemnation for those who are in Christ Jesus. —Romans 8:1 NIV

In the days we are living, we need to recognize our battle is not with flesh and blood. Even though we see people doing all kinds of dark, horrendous, and evil acts, we need to understand that people are not our enemies.

It's time to live in the light. It's time to love one another from pure hearts and with pure motives. Intercession is all about bringing the Kingdom together and healing the places where the enemy has lied and sown division. It's about healing the hearts of individuals, people groups, cities, nations, and beyond. Our role is to partner with the Lord and put things right in the world. We need to go back to the Garden and God's original intent, partnering with Him to care for His creation. We must rise up and recognize that we carry the light of God inside of us. And it was said of Jesus,

> In Him was life, and the life was the Light of men.
> ... There was the true Light which, coming into the
> world, enlightens every man.   —John 1:4,9

We can release light into every dark place and forbid darkness to operate. We can be the light of hope that destroys the lies of the enemy. We can be a team of champions who are, as Bob Hartley says, "Joyful Comrades." We can become the Lovelutionaries that are part of the great love awakening, being revolutionaries of the Kingdom of life and light. It is our finest hour. Let's stop pointing fingers at others and look to the Lord for fresh oil from heaven to fill our lampstands so we can see like an owl in the dark and spot the enemy that is coming against us. We can wrestle and overthrow the works

Intercession is all about bringing the Kingdom together and healing the places where the enemy has lied and sown division. It's about healing the hearts of individuals, people groups, cities, nations, and beyond.

of darkness when we become one with God, who longs for all to come to Him and find life!

I was on a mission trip in Brazil a few years ago. One day as we were leaving the church where we had been ministering, I heard this horrid demonic mocking laugh. "What is that?" I asked the Holy Spirit. He told me it was a mocking spirit and He took me to look out over the balcony. I saw people gathered around a young woman, declaring, "More, Lord!" I felt the Lord's grief over the lack of discernment operating, but I could not do anything about it because our buses were leaving.

Once we were back on our bus, I prayed for freedom for this woman with the mocking spirit. I also talked with the Lord about the whole situation, asking Him why the people praying over her did not discern that the young woman's manifestation was not from Him, but the enemy instead. He shared that there are times we are so afraid to grieve Him that we forget to ask Him if He is moving or if there's another spirit operating. When God moves, the enemy sows His tares also. He did not want this woman to be free, so when the demonic spirit began to manifest, it manifested in similar ways to the manifestations of Holy Spirit.

We do not need to be concerned or afraid, we only to need to be tender and yielded to God. We must always stay in a position of asking Him questions, remaining teachable. As He teaches us, we must love those whom the enemy has bound up. God allows us to see the work of the enemy so we can set His children free.

A few days later we were back at the same church. During worship I heard that mocking laugh again and I asked the Lord, "What do You want me to do, Lord?"

He sent me into the sanctuary to stand in the back behind the worshippers and He showed me where this woman with the mocking spirit was standing. Then He instructed me to go stand behind her. When I did, He had me release His love and peace over her. It was incredible to feel it rise up in me and flow out to her. She was waving a flag over people, and suddenly she turned around and looked at me. The Lord instructed me to take her in my arms and release His love. I did. She fell out in the Spirit into His love and rest. I prayed over her, then over the ones around her. After a time, I left her in His presence and went to the back of the sanctuary to watch and pray.

At the end of worship, she found me. Through a translator she asked me if what she was doing was from the Lord. I asked her if she really wanted to know and she said, "Yes." Because of her *yes*, I told her it was not from the Lord and asked her if she would like to be set free. I found another team member and together we ministered to her. As she submitted to the Lord, she was gloriously set free! I saw her the next day in worship and the light and life of God were shining out of her.

Because I submitted to God's strategy, I was able to see that I had not been wrestling with her but with the demonic force trying to operate through her. This demon was counterfeiting the authentic move of Holy Spirit and mocking the living God by getting people to agree with its agenda. With God's strategy to release His love light and His peace, she was open to being set free. Darkness met light and it had to flee. In God's presence she felt safe and was able to receive her healing.

God is safe! Whether it is intercession, healing, or deliverance, the ministry of the Lord will leave the one being ministered to feeling loved and safe. Love is the most powerful force and it is the safety shield that will draw people to Him so they can be set free.

We, the church, must recognize that the enemy is a warfare strategist. He has strongholds and lies to keep us from walking with the very ones we are called to be with. He knows that if he can bring division to divine alignments, he will keep us from being the synergistic powerful worshipping army that can displace him in a region. When we engage in battle we need discernment, not suspicion.

True discernment recognizes the gift of God in someone even when they are not fully walking in it. True discernment recognizes that there are not just evil spirits operating among us, but God and His Spirit and His heavenly host are also working among us. When we walk in true and pure discernment, we will partner with the Kingdom of Light and not the kingdom of darkness.

I have been in meetings and have heard the voice of the enemy whispering his poisonous lies into the ears of anyone who will listen. At one such time I almost fell prey to his lies. Even today, I am grieved by how I was almost deceived, but I'm thankful that in that wrestling match, the Lord and I won and a curse was broken off one my dearest covenant friends.

It happened when I was ministering with my friend. She and I had prepared together by going on retreat. We spent a great deal of time in prayer and received clear revelation and insight, and a commissioning from the Lord. He released His angels on assignment to be our ministry team. Hebrews says:

> Are not all angels ministering spirits sent to serve those who will inherit salvation?
>
> —Hebrews 1:14 NIV

We were excited with the promises, the instructions, and the divine revelation the Lord gave us. The trip was better than we could have hoped for. The Lord was true to His Word and released His host among us to minister and empower. The release of heaven was tangible, powerful, and life-changing for many.

The last night of the conference it was my friend's turn to speak. She is a dynamic woman of God who carries His glory and presence. She releases revelation from heaven that instructs us in how to walk in this life. She is a true covenant friend. That night she danced a dance from heaven before she spoke, and the presence of God was glorious. As soon as she began to speak I heard the most negative thoughts about her and about what she was speaking. I literally had to wrestle those thoughts and take them captive, as Paul instructed us in Corinthians:

> We demolish arguments and every pretension that sets itself up against the knowledge of God, and we take captive every thought to make it obedient to Christ.   —2 Corinthians 10:5 NIV

I had to battle in prayer the entire time she spoke. I had never encountered anything this strong before. I called on Father to release heaven through her and bind those thoughts. Even though I knew they were not my thoughts or how I perceived her and the ministry she was releasing, I still had to battle intensely because the lies were fierce. My position was two-fold: to cry out to Father to release heaven to my friend, and through her to bind the enemy's assault. At the end of her message she had a powerful call to the people and wanted me to join her. I was still trying to discern what was taking place at that point and didn't want to taint the call, so I stood back to pray instead.

That night after the meeting, when she and I talked through what had happened, we realized that there had been a demonic assignment to set up a stronghold around her that would change how people perceived her. It was very painful to process what had happened, but the test has a powerful testimony. Because we were faithful to battle through until we heard God's voice, He enabled us to tear down the enemy's stronghold, giving us wisdom to teach people not to come into agreement with the enemy's lies.

When I returned to my home church after our trip together, the first Sunday during worship I heard voices saying negative things about the worship and the leaders. Because I had already been instructed by God about this particular way in which the enemy tries to deceive with his lies, I knew exactly what was going on and was able to intercede and break the enemy's hold. The enemy was speaking to the people to try to get them to turn away from the very place they were called by God to be. He was attempting to bring division, to release an orphan spirit, to release bitter-root judgments and negative agreements. Who we agree with is who we empower.

Let me share from the Word the revelation that came out of this and what the Father has taught me about wrestling to win. In 2 Corinthians it says,

> For though we live in the world, we do not wage war as the world does. The weapons we fight with are not the weapons of the world. On the contrary, they have divine power to demolish strongholds [fortresses]. We demolish arguments and every pretension that sets itself up against the knowledge of God, and we take captive every thought to make it obedient to Christ. And we will be ready to punish every act of disobedience, once your obedience is complete.
>
> —2 Corinthians 10:3-6 NIV

Strong's Concordance gives us a definition for the word *fortress* as used in verse 4: "strongholds of the arguments and reasonings by which a disputant endeavors to fortify

We have been given the keys to the Kingdom and we are to use them to open up and to lock up. With the keys to the Kingdom we can unlock the release of heaven, blocking the enemy's access into our lives and the lives of the ones we stand with and pray for.

his opinion and defend it against his opponent."[1] In other words, the enemy builds up strongholds and prisons around people that he wants us to see them through. His goal is to change our perception of others by releasing lies about them that sound reasonable. He does this to try and fortify or strengthen his warfare against God's anointed.

That is why it is so important that we realize whom we are wrestling with. If we are wrestling with God for a blessing, then we should press on. But when we are wrestling with the enemy to defeat him, we need to ask, seek, and knock on the door of heaven in order to get God's strategy.

Remember, we have been given all authority to bind and loose, to lock and unlock. We have been given the keys to the Kingdom and we are to use them to open up and to lock up. With the keys to the Kingdom we can unlock the release of heaven, blocking the enemy's access into our lives and the lives of the ones we stand with and pray for. We can lock the enemy out. We have the keys to tear down and forbid every stronghold. And we have the keys to give the Lord access into

[1] Strong, James. *The New Strong's Expanded Exhaustive Concordance of the Bible*, Nashville: Thomas Nelson, 2010.

our lives. We have the keys to open up the gates of heaven and let the King of Glory come into every place we desire for Him to move!

I have had the privilege of ministering in churches that truly carry the Kingdom heart of God, and the love and the unity is empowering. Oh, that they could walk in what they have all their days! This is why I go where the Father sends me, to teach and share the revelations that He has given me. I am hopeful about His church. I believe that the body of Christ should be the safest place in the world. I have seen the awakening going on in the church. Many have been pressing into what God is doing through them over the past few years.

I have seen a love movement beginning to shake and quake the systems of this world. Chains are falling off, eyes are opening, and hearts are healing, awakening, and surrendering to the God of Love. I see fear and suspicion replaced with love and compassion. I am hopeful that Jesus will have His Lovelution! I want us to take this verse from Colossians:

> Epaphras, who is one of you and a servant of Christ Jesus, sends greetings. He is always wrestling in prayer for you, that you may stand firm in all the will of God, mature and fully assured.
>
> —Colossians 4:12 NIV

And make it into a prayer:

> *I, who am one with the body of the Lord and servant of Christ Jesus, send greetings of hope and peace. I will wrestle in prayer for the body of believers, that they may stand firm in all the will of God, mature and fully assured.*

7

Breaking the Fear Barrier

When I am afraid, I will trust in you.

—Psalm 56:3 NIV

TO BE AN INTREPID WARRIOR and live a life of fearless intercession, we must annihilate fear. We cannot allow fear to gain any foothold in us. We must be free from every root of fear, and when fear does come, we must go to the Lord in faith and receive the power to break through the fear barrier. I've heard people say that if you are afraid to do something and know you are supposed to do it, then do it afraid.

When I first began as an intercessor, I tried over and over to live out that saying but often found myself paralyzed by fear. Very little fruit came from operating in my own strength. Then God gave me the revelation to call on Him and to trust in Him to deliver me from fear and to help me in every situation. As I learned to trust God in the midst of fear, I began to see fruit flow from my efforts.

If we agree with fear, we open the door to dread. Job 3:25 NAS reads, *"For what I fear comes upon me, and what I dread befalls me."* Fear and dread block our access to heavenly places in Christ, literally pulling us out of faith and into a pit of hopelessness. Fear is a dark cloud that blocks out the light of truth. As intrepid warriors we must live without fear, as bold and fearless intercessors. We have the answer to cast out all fear, to walk in discernment, to live in peace, and to walk fully in all God has given us. The answer is in Him and His love. There are many keys to the power of love in 1 John 4:

> Beloved, do not believe every spirit, but test the spirits to see whether they are from God, because many false prophets have gone out into the world. By this you know the Spirit of God: every spirit that confesses that Jesus Christ has come in the flesh is from God; and every spirit that does not confess Jesus is not from God ; this is the spirit of the antichrist, of which you have heard that it is coming, and now it is already in the world. You are from God, little children, and have overcome them; because greater is He who is in you than he who is in the world. They are from the world; therefore they speak as from the world, and the world listens to them. We are from God; he who knows God listens to us; he who is not from God does not listen to us. By this we know the spirit of truth and

the spirit of error. Beloved, let us love one another, for love is from God; and everyone who loves is born of God and knows God. —1 John 4:1-7

We have come to know and have believed the love which God has for us. God is love, and the one who abides in love abides in God, and God abides in him. By this, love is perfected with us, so that we may have confidence in the day of judgment; because as He is, so also are we in this world. There is no fear in love; but perfect love casts out fear, because fear involves punishment, and the one who fears is not perfected in love. We love, because He first loved us.

1 John 4:16-19

In these verses John is instructing us to test every spirit. How do we do that? We test everything through love. He is also reminding us that Jesus has overcome the world. Verse 17 tells us that as Jesus is in the world, so are we. This is good news! Verse 18 says there is no fear or punishment in love. Perfect love casts out all fear. When we abide in Jesus and His love, we live without fear. When we live without fear, we live in peace with God and man. There should be no fear of man in us and no fear of the enemy, because God is for us. Perfect love makes us overcomers.

But in all these things we overwhelmingly conquer through Him who loved us. For I am convinced that neither death, nor life, nor angels, nor principalities, nor things present, nor things to come, nor powers, nor height, nor depth, nor any other created thing, will be able to separate us from the love of God, which is in Christ Jesus our Lord.

—Romans 8:37-39

The Power of Agreement to Dismantle Fear

Agreement between two faith-filled believers can dismantle fear. There is great power available when we agree in faith together for what we are praying. Sometimes as I pray for situations, the spirit of fear will try to intimidate me. There have been times when a demonic entity has appeared and tried to get me to back down. One such time was in India. I was asleep in my hotel room and the Lord woke me up and told me to look up. When I did I saw dark eerie demonic faces leering at me. I told them to "go in Jesus' name." At the same time this was happening to me, the Lord woke up a team member, Joyce Farinato, who saw the very same thing. The Lord told her to pray for me. Later that morning I praised the Lord with song and dance to dismantle the enemy's schemes.

I have learned to pay attention to the many ways God reveals His heart for breakthrough. We must learn how to know Him to the fullest extent possible. He is brilliant, radiant, and multi-faceted, and He loves for us to seek out the mysteries of heaven. Intercession can be prayers prayed, words declared through decrees and through proclamations and declarations, and it can also be poems, songs, dance, and every form of the arts. God is very creative. The arts are powerful prophetic acts that release the power of God. I have had

I have learned to pay attention to the many ways God reveals His heart for breakthrough. We must learn how to know Him to the fullest extent possible. He is brilliant, radiant, and multi-faceted, and He loves for us to seek out the mysteries of heaven.

many artists paint the breakthrough in intercession gatherings.

The following is a testimony from my friend Mary Hasz in which she shares how revelatory prophetic art released the power of agreement. I was praying against a death threat over someone's life. The Lord alerted Mary so she could join with me in intercession.

I was sitting in the Presence in my sunroom. My lower back began to hurt. I looked out my window at the clouds and saw one very near that looked just like a skull. Just in front of it was a very small cloud that looked like a seahorse. I asked Holy Spirit what was going on, and He said, "Tracee Anne is in warfare." My phone immediately rang. It was Tracee Anne. She said, "How are you?" I asked, "What are you warring against?" She asked, "How do you know that?" I answered, "My lower back hurts, and I am looking at a cloud that is shaped like a skull." She replied, "Oh! You're looking at the spirit of death!" I said, "So that's what that is!" She replied, "I am in prayer for someone who has a death threat against their life."

"At this point Tracee Anne and I came into agreement prayer to cancel the death assignment over this person. During the prayer, she began decreeing, "I take out an arrow and shoot it at the spirit of death." She declared this over and over. When we got off the phone, Holy Spirit instructed me to go outside and take a picture of that cloud. I said, "I don't want to go anywhere near it," and did not take the picture. As I watched, the skull cloud folded in on itself and was gone. The next morning when I awoke, I saw in the spirit realm an archer shooting arrows at a skull. Holy Spirit instructed me to get up and paint what I saw. I said, "Lord, I've never painted a skull!" He said, "Yes, your job will be more difficult because you did not take the photo." I set up my easel and canvas.

Tracee Anne had sent me a link to Kim Clement's website. He released a prophetic word that the enemy was causing unnatural deaths coming against the body. While listening to the worship from his broadcast and the prophetic prayers he prayed, I partnered with Holy Spirit and put on canvas the prophetic picture I saw of the intrepid warrior shooting arrows at the spirit of death and bringing victory.

When two people come together and agree with God's heart, God empowers our intercession with His breaker anointing. The schemes of the enemy failed and God prevailed! Hallelujah!

The Power of Love to Conquer Fear

Nothing is more powerful than the love of God. The fire of God's love burns up every yoke of the enemy, routing out the evil one who would hide.

> Put me like a seal over your heart, like a seal on your arm. For love is as strong as death, jealousy is as severe as Sheol; its flashes are flashes of fire, the very flame of the Lord. Many waters cannot quench love, nor will rivers overflow it; if a man were to give all the riches of his house for love, it would be utterly despised.
> —Song of Solomon 8:6-7

Love-powered prayers released through the heart of a Lovelutionary follower of Jesus are like fiery missiles that act with a targeted precision to destroy the dark schemes of the enemy. God's love is the most powerful force there is. The fire of God's love is stronger than death, and the One who holds the keys to life and death is "Love" Himself.

A hug can be a love-powered prayer that changes someone's life. I know this from personal experience. I was in Las Vegas once when Heidi Baker was ministering. At one point she asked those called to the nations to come up front, and I went forward. Heidi went down the row praying for each person, and when she got to me she simply held me, praying that the Father's love would go deeper into me. She also prayed that I would be able to pray simple prayers. As she held me, I felt my heart shatter. Hardness and fear broke as His love poured into me. I experienced a heart transplant that forever changed me. Love broke in and now love pours out. Today my prayer life is simple, filled with faith, hope and love. When I pray, the power of Jehovah Ahava - God is love - pours out of me, burning down walls and releasing His Kingdom of holy love. Love overcomes all fear!

> Blow them away like smoke. Melt them like wax in a fire. Let the wicked perish in the presence of God.
> —Psalm 68:2 NLT

The fire of God's love also exposes the enemy and his schemes. It will route out every demon that is hiding and break every curse. When I was in South Africa, a leader shared with me that right before they begin the harvest they set a low fire and watch over it. This fire burns out all the snakes and varmints, making it safe for the workers to come and gather in the harvest. The fire of God is like this harvest fire. When His holy fire comes, the enemy scatters! *"For the Lord your God is a consuming fire, a jealous God"* (Deuteronomy 4:24).

His Protection and Provision Break Fear

Fearless breakthrough also comes when we partner with God's protection and His provision of angels who watch over us. One of God's names is Jehovah Sabaoth, which means "Lord of the Angel Armies." Many times in the Bible, angels appear and announce, "Do not be afraid." We can be secure in the knowledge that God and His heavenly host are greater and bigger than the enemy's force.

Fearless breakthrough also comes when we partner with God's protection and His provision of angels who watch over us. One of God's names is Jehovah Sabaoth, which means "Lord of the Angel Armies."

He who dwells in the shelter of the Most High will abide in the shadow of the Almighty. I will say to the Lord, "My refuge and my fortress, my God, in whom I trust!" For it is He who delivers you from the snare of the trapper and from the deadly pestilence. He will cover you with His pinions, And under His wings you may seek refuge; His faithfulness is a shield and bulwark.

You will not be afraid of the terror by night, or of the arrow that flies by day; of the pestilence that stalks in darkness, or of the destruction that lays waste at noon. A thousand may fall at your side and ten thousand at your right hand, but it shall not approach you. You will only look on with your eyes and see the recompense of the wicked. For you have made the Lord, my refuge, even the Most High, your dwelling place. No evil will befall you, nor will any plague come near your tent.

For He will give His angels charge concerning you, to guard you in all your ways. They will bear you up in their hands, that you do not strike your foot against a stone. You will tread upon the lion and cobra, the young lion and the serpent you will trample down.

Because he has loved Me, therefore I will deliver him; I will set him securely on high, because he has known My name. He will call upon Me, and I will answer him; I will be with him in trouble; I will rescue him and honor him. With a long life I will satisfy him and let him see My salvation.

—Psalm 91

This is a beautiful Psalm that speaks of the protection of the Most High. We need to understand how the love of God shines through His heart and that He created angels to protect us, deliver us, bring messages to us, and cause His plans to happen.

God's Word also tells us in Psalm 103:20, *"Bless the Lord, you His angels, mighty in strength, who perform His word, obeying the voice of His word!"*

The first chapter of Hebrews tells of the ministry of Jesus in comparison to the ministry of angels, and verse 14 says that angels are ministering spirits sent to render service for those who inherit salvation. Praise God that He has made protective provision for us so we can break through every fear barrier!

I was very afraid when I embarked on my first ministry trip outside the United States. I was afraid of the unknown and all kinds of things, because of the stories missionaries had shared in church. People kept cautioning me to watch out for this and that, and eventually fear took root in my heart. However, as I shared in Chapter 2, while I sat in the airport talking to the Lord, a feather fell into my lap and He spoke Psalm 91 to me, assuring me that when I was in His will I was safe because He was with me, and His provision of angelic protection was also with me.

I had many encounters with the Lord on that trip and also experienced His angelic provision, with signs and wonders following. Since then I have not experienced the paralyzing fear that had tried to keep me home or make me ineffective. Because of God's definite signs of protection and confirmation through His Word, I am able to run with Him wherever He sends me.

A revelation of Holy Spirit as the fiery power inside of us that helps us to walk with God as overcomers will also enable us to break through the fear barrier. I was in Moravian Falls one spring, wrestling with a difficult situation, when I had an encounter with an angel. Whether I was awake or asleep, I do not know. As I was resting, an angel of the Lord came into my room and sat at the end of my bed. He took my hand and began to pour oil into me, and as he did I heard in my innermost being that peace was being released to me to walk through this situation.

I knew God was with me. I felt saturated in the peaceful presence of God and my prayers shifted after this encounter.

The light of God that flowed through this angel shined deep into the darkness of the situation, allowing me to see God's perspective. Everything shifted into heaven's view, and God worked it all out for His good.

On another occasion I found myself again in Moravian Falls, on a personal retreat. I didn't know it at the time, but a huge breakthrough was to occur in my life on this retreat. I thought my assignment was to write, and I did some writing, but there was more for me than writing. I was going to learn how to break through the fear barrier by abiding deeper in the Spirit of the Lord. His provision broke the fear.

On the first night, I was fasting and praying and the Lord instructed me to fast from talking. I thought a silent fast would be easy because I was by myself. Alone in a beautiful cabin, expectant for heavenly encounters, I got terror and warfare instead. The wind was terrible that night, howling and banging against the walls of the cabin, creating a hellish symphony of sounds that brought great fear to my heart. Throughout the dark hours of that night I experienced the presence and provision of the Lord as He delivered me of fear and taught me how to pray from my spirit to silence fear. I learned to commune with Him in a place of trust and confidence by facing the demonic realm from my spirit. Because of my commitment to fast from talking, I wrestled through the night in silence, calling out to God from my soul and spirit, crying out for His help. I was able to come into a place of trust and peace with God that has forever marked my life and

When we refuse to agree with fear and instead agree with
God, in love joining our prayers of intercession with others,
we will see the mighty power of God break every chain.
Jesus is the man of war.

ministry. Now I can pray from my spirit in situations where I
cannot speak out loud.

One such situation happened on a Global Awakening
ministry trip to Brazil. I was praying with a team member
when someone from another team came to tell me that witchcraft was being released over the prayer team, and the person
doing it was sitting near me. I sensed fear trying to take hold.
I began to release peace and asked Holy Spirit what to do. He
said to pray from spirit, extend my hand toward the person
in a way that would not be discerned, and bind the works of
witchcraft, calling for the person to repent or leave. I did this
and the person left.

Many times I have had to pray through situations that
could have had a dramatically different outcome had I been
praying from a place of fear. I have seen the terrible, frightening
demonic beings that torment God's created people, and
was terrified myself by these beings until I came into the
fullness of the revelation of God's great and powerful
protective love. When we receive strategies from heaven, we
will be empowered with bold faith and confidence in God's

greatness, and will be able to access His resources. When we refuse to agree with fear and instead agree with God, in love joining our prayers of intercession with others, we will see the mighty power of God break every chain. Jesus is the man of war.

> Therefore He is able also to save forever those who draw near to God through Him, since He always lives to make intercession for them.
>
> —Hebrews 7:25

8

The Message of Breakthrough

Many are the afflictions of the righteous, but the Lord delivers him out of them all.   —Psalm 34:19

THERE IS A PROMISE OF BREAKTHROUGH, a message of breakthrough that tells us that the Lord delivers the righteous from all afflictions. When we step into this revelation from the Holy Spirit, we can experience personal and corporate breakthrough in intercession, because when God gives us revelation, He backs it up with His power.

In order to experience His breakthrough, we need to see things from our place of being seated with Christ in heavenly places (Ephesians 2:6). We pray to God and believe in faith from our identity in Christ. What holds us back from breakthrough? What keeps us from breaking out? Why are we not breaking forth into our inheritance in Christ? The message of breakthrough for me was formed in the fire of intimacy with the Lord as I asked Him these questions, and my testimony is that God's revelation is true – we are to partner with the Lord, who is the breaker.

We have been given the ability to *break through* the chains of bondage, to *break out* of old mindsets, so we may *break forth* and be rightly connected to the vine of Christ. Through our fearless intercession, we can help others move out of their hard places so they too can leave behind old patterns and come forth into the glory of the Lord. We can all step over the threshold and into our destiny and into fullness in Him.

> The breaker goes up before them; they break out, pass through the gate and go out by it. So their king goes on before them, and the Lord at their head.
> —Micah 2:13 NAS

The breaker anointing is powerful, and the concepts I am going to present in this chapter are simple springboards to propel you into the fullness of God. The Lord of the breakthrough is able to break us out of strongholds so we can come forth and remain firmly in His faith, hope, and love, which will produce great joy and peace in our lives.

Our intercession can bring us, along with others including churches, workplaces, cities, and nations, into the promises of God. When we know the Lord's voice and come into agreement with His heart, the possibilities are endless.

The Power of the Trinity

It is important to understand that as intercessors we need to live in oneness with the Father, the Son and the Holy Spirit – the Holy Three, the Trinity.

> And if one can overpower him who is alone, two can resist him. A cord of three strands is not quickly torn apart. —Ecclesiastes 4:12

When we stand with the Lord, who is the eternal three-fold cord, we will not be torn apart. He is our keeping power. *"The Lord is your keepe"* (Psalm 121:5). He brings us into the unity of the Spirit. He wraps us up into Himself, backs us up when we are in agreement with His promises, and shatters the barriers that hold us back. When we discover the beauty of unity in the power of three, we will experience a "wonder and awe breakthrough."

> Therefore I, the prisoner of the Lord, implore you to walk in a manner worthy of the calling with which you have been called, with all humility and gentleness, with patience, showing tolerance for one another in love, being diligent to preserve the unity of the Spirit in the bond of peace. There is one body and one Spirit, just as also you were called in one hope of your calling; one Lord, one faith, one baptism, one God and Father of all who is over all and through all and in all. —Ephesians 4:1-6

The Power of Faith, Hope, and Love

As intercessors, when we take hold of faith, hope, and love, we are empowered by the three substances of the Kingdom of God that will always get us into the right place. They are impartations from God and pieces of the heavenly map that lead us into realms of breakthrough and into a greater ability to live a life of fearless intercession. *"But now faith, hope, love, abide these three; but the greatest of these is love"* (1 Corinthians 13:13). We will see walls come down and barriers removed when we are empowered by faith, hope, and love.

Faith to Break Through

When we receive the gift of faith from God in intercession, this powerful substance of Kingdom will dispel fear, unbelief and doubt, and remove all hindrances and barriers to God's will. *"Now faith is the substance of things hoped for, the evidence of things not seen"* (Hebrews 11:1 NKJV). As intercessors, we must live a life of faith. We must live on a rock of faith in order to be used by God to move mountains.

Faith is mentioned 228 times in the New Testament and is described in the Greek Lexicon as "belief, trust, and loyalty to a person or thing."[2] There are many places in our journey with God where we can receive faith to break through, but it is important that we understand that how we receive faith from God plays an important role in how we partner with Him. *"Now faith is the assurance of things hoped for, the conviction of things not seen"* (Hebrews 11:1).

[2] J.H. Thayer, Greek-English Lexicon of the New Testament (Grand Rapids: Michigan, 1977)

As intercessors, when we take hold of faith, hope, and love,
we are empowered by the three substances of the Kingdom
of God that will always get us into the right place.

I received the gift of faith mentioned in 1 Corinthians 12:9 from the Lord Jesus when He came into an intercessory prayer gathering I was leading. As we were praying, He spoke to me and said to ask everyone to kneel. We all knelt and then He instructed me to put out my hands. As I obeyed Him I felt something weighty come into my hands. When I asked Him what it was, He responded, "This is the gift of faith. Freely you receive, freely give. You may impart this gift when I instruct you to." Since that time I have seen faith, as the power of God, cause mountains and obstacles to be moved out of the way and replaced by the Kingdom of God.

When we follow the Lord's leading, we will feel the substance of faith and see the working of that faith move mountains. I have seen this in my own life many times. A few years ago, I had just returned from a ministry trip and was having dinner with my family when I heard the Lord instruct me to call my sister and pray for the baby in my niece's womb. Following the Lord's leading, I called immediately. As we spoke on the phone, I was led to ask them to place the receiver near my niece's abdomen so I could prophetically decree, by faith, what the Lord was showing me. It was a time of powerful and purposeful prayer.

In my personal prayer time two mornings later, I had a vision of the baby in the womb with the umbilical cord wrapped around him, trying to strangle him. As I asked the Lord how to pray, He revealed to me a generational curse that was manifesting. He then showed me how to pray by faith in agreement with Him, decreeing that by His faith and the power of the blood of Jesus this curse was cancelled.

Two days later my niece went into labor. There were problems and my sister called asking for prayer. I was able immediately to move into prayer with great faith to cancel the plans of the enemy, because the Lord had already led me in prayer to break the curse and prophesy destiny over this child. My daughters were praying with me and we agreed that the plans of the Lord for this child would come forth. The peace of the Lord came on us all.

A few hours later my sister called to say that the baby had arrived and was fine. She said the nurse was calling it a miracle because the umbilical cord had wrapped itself around his neck and belly and was strangling him with every push from his mother throughout the labor. My beautiful, brilliant little nephew is alive today and filled with the sounds of heaven waiting to be released, because of the gift of faith that worked through us.

Hope to Break Out

Jesus is the door of hope and I believe many are awakening to this revelation, to a clearer understanding of who we are in Christ and who He is in us. As this revelation takes up residence in our hearts, we can walk through the open door of hope and take hold of the power of God available to us there.

> So Jesus said to them again, "Truly, truly, I say to you, I am the door of the sheep. All who came before Me are thieves and robbers, but the sheep did not hear them. I am the door; if anyone enters through Me, he will be saved, and will go in and out and find pasture."   —John 10:7-9

Often it's difficult to get across the threshold. The enemy will do everything he can to deceive us into believing that the door is locked and we can't gain access. We need to press in with faithful devotion to seek Jesus who is the Door and who is behind the door and who holds the keys to the Kingdom. In the midst of our struggles, our loving Father will call us into the wilderness and with compassion give us the valley of Achor as a door of hope, saying, "You are my people!" If we persevere in hope, travailing as if in the final stages of child-birth, the Father will bring forth what is inside of us. He will enable us to soar on the very storm winds sent to destroy us.

> Restore to me the joy of Your salvation and sustain me with a willing spirit.   —Psalm 51:12

As intercessors, we can carry others into the realms of God's heart and bring them into the presence of the personification of hope, which is Jesus Christ.

When we receive the mighty substance of faith from God, it will lead us to hope, which will then empower us to break free of restrictive situations and hindrances and into God's increase. It is hope that leads us out of distorted mindsets of discouragement, despair and the heart sickness that comes when hope is deferred. Hope that is based on God – knowing Him, spending time with Him – takes us out of wrong thinking and into a place of trust in God. When we stand in a place of hope, we can take hold of the power of God's love. One of the best ways to get hope is to give it away. Outward focus rather than inward focus will bring faith to us and to others.

A wrong focus on self, especially self-introspection that looks for perceived flaws and weaknesses, will lead us away from hope. Instead of a wrong focus, we need to fix our eyes on Jesus, the author and perfecter of our faith (Hebrews 12:2) and on His sufficient grace working in us. My personal definition of "to break forth" is "to blossom, grow and become who we are created to be." Faith means agreeing with the Lord about who He says we are. When we live in faith, we will be transformed from glory to glory by the power of His love.

> Therefore, having been justified by faith, we have peace with God through our Lord Jesus Christ, through whom also we have obtained our introduction by faith into this grace in which we stand; and we exult in hope of the glory of God. And not only this, but we also exult in our tribulations, knowing that tribulation

brings about perseverance; and perseverance, proven character; and proven character, hope; and hope does not disappoint, because the love of God has been poured out within our hearts through the Holy Spirit who was given to us. —Romans 5:1-5

Love – The Door to the Father's Heart

But the greatest of these is love.
—1 Corinthians 13:13 NIV

God is love and Jesus is the door to the Father's heart of love. When we come into the place of knowing we are loved and nothing can ever separate us from God's love, we release heaven everywhere we go.

Beloved, let us love one another, for love is from God; and everyone who loves is born of God and knows God. The one who does not love does not know God, for God is love. By this the love of God was manifested in us, that God has sent His only begotten Son into the world so that we might live through Him. In this is love, not that we loved God, but that He loved us and sent His Son to be the propitiation for our sins. Beloved, if God so loved us, we also ought to love one another. No one has seen God at any time; if we love one another, God abides in us, and His love is perfected in us. By this we know that we abide in Him and He in us, because He has given us of His Spirit. —1 John 4:7-13

Love is the greatest commandment. When we break forth in love, we break forth into joy.

> "You shall love the Lord your God with all your heart, and with all your soul, and with all your mind." This is the great and foremost commandment. The second is like it: "You shall love your neighbor as yourself."
>
> —Matthew 22:37-39

The glory of God is His loving-kindness. His glory-love transforms us into His image, making us like Him.

> We all, who with unveiled faces contemplate the Lord's glory, are being transformed into his image with ever-increasing glory, which comes from the Lord, who is the Spirit.   —2 Corinthians 3:18 NIV

Faith is God's gift to us.

Jesus is the door of hope.

God is the fullness and essence of love.

Jesus told His followers to beware of the leaven of the Pharisees and Herod. What He was speaking about was a religious and political leaven that kills the spirit. This is not a love-based leaven, but a law – a man-pleasing, self-promoting and image-protecting leaven that has no place in the Kingdom of heaven.

As intercessors, we want the leaven of love. We need love to permeate everything we say, everything we do, and everything we pray. Love never fails. If we stand in the gap with love, God will never fail us. But if we stand in the gap for others with the law, we will not bring hope. We will not be able to bring the freedom and the peace that are part of the Kingdom. If we stand in the gap with a man-pleasing attitude in our heart, we will only pray, say, and do what we think others believe to be acceptable. If we stand in the gap wanting to be seen, for someone to notice us, and to gain position in the eyes of men because of our spiritual prowess, we will have lost the focus of the cross. Those who love will lay down their lives for a friend. Jesus wants all mankind to be His friends. He gave His life for all. We must remember that prayers prayed from the heart of love never fail. Be like Christ when it comes to love and life! Jesus is our model. Pray like He prayed; follow His lead.

When Breakthrough, Breakout, and Break Forth Happen

There is a level of faith we can step into right now that has not been available to us before. There is a *breakthrough* coming that will release a crazy praise that will cause the atmosphere around us to shake and release treasures from the

As intercessors we want the leaven of love. We need love to permeate everything we say, everything we do, and everything we pray. Love never fails. If we stand in the gap with love, God will never fail us.

darkness. It will shine forth with the glory of heaven. Can you feel it? Can you see it? Will we believe it and receive it? Now is our time, our chance to say, "Do it again, Lord; break through for us as you have for others!" I believe this breakout will bring the greatest release of creativity yet seen.

As director of intercession for Global Awakening, I have personally experienced breakthrough, breakout and break forth. In 2012, my team of intercessors and I began a time of pressing heaven for promises and prophetic words. One of my prayer partners and I had been praying, agreeing, and believing God for a million dollar breakthrough offering.

Before one service, the Lord had me break curses off Randy Clark and Tom Jones, the Executive Director of Global Awakening, and to release them from everything hindering them from moving forward. Tom asked me to pray we make budget, and I told him in faith to add zeros to that need. In the offering we found a prophetic check for $1,000,000 that had been drawn by a little child. The power of prophetic release and agreement were flowing from many places!

As we gathered for our spring network meeting, the Voice of the Prophets Conference, the warfare was fierce, but God stood up as our dread champion, the Breaker, and opened up the realm of miraculous possibilities. Words of knowledge regarding a large, million-dollar offering came forth from one of our speakers, and the offering from the Friday evening service was indeed over one million dollars! The prophetic decrees from the prophet and the prayers of the intercessors collided with faith, and God did what only God can do.

The joy of this breakthrough was close to the joy of a new birth. When I first heard the news I had to run outside to shout, praise, and spin in delight as tears of joy fell down my cheeks. And now I want to shout this testimony from the rooftops, because Revelation 19:10 says, "For the testimony of Jesus is the spirit of prophecy."

In July of 2012, I saw the Lord move powerfully again as He released His faith, hope and love over thousands of young people. I was with Global Awakening's training team in Brasilia, Brazil, for their Youth Power Invasion event. The first night, God released His faith as we heard the sounds of angels singing praises with us. Many were healed that night. The second night, God released His hope as He broke the chains of heart sickness. Many were saved, healed, delivered, and baptized in Holy Spirit and fire. On the third night, we saw God's glory breaking forth as He filled the house and showered us with His transforming love.

I was asked to speak for each of these three nights as a result of a prophetic word that came in a dream to a woman named Dani Rocha. The church where I was to speak had been through many tough times and was crying out for a breakthrough.

The first night, the Lord came in glory as my translator and I sang in the Spirit. You could feel the shift of heaven come into the atmosphere as people heard the angels singing harmony with us. That night the youth team prayed for the sick and saw healings and miracles, some for the very first time.

The second night, I released a prophetic word of hope and healing as I shared about the baptism of the Holy Spirit and fire. At the end of the evening the altar was full with people giving their lives to Jesus. Many were baptized in the Holy Spirit and fire, and again we witnessed many healings.

On the third night, we experienced a glorious third-day resurrection power breaking forth as a cloud of the Shekinah glory of the Lord came into the meeting. His glory was seen by the children, the youth, and the adults as we all entered into high and loving praise. God healed His people, and His glory was on us that night. The power of God's presence is truly fullness of joy.

I believe we are at the precipice of breakthrough in the body of Christ. In Deuteronomy 1:11 we are told that twelve spies were sent in the Promised Land and only two believed with eyes of faith what the Lord spoke to them. *"May the Lord, God of your fathers, increase you a thousand-fold more than you are and bless you, just as He has promised you!"*

Whose report will we believe? Are we in the ranks of the ten or the two? Do we have faith to believe for our breakthrough so we can break out of every old pattern and break forth into the glory of the Lord? As we pray and agree with God, He is releasing all of heaven so that His purposes and dreams can be released into the earth.

God has put dreams inside each one of us. He has abundance laid up for us, treasuries of resources in heaven, and we are His advocates here on earth standing in the gap so that His Kingdom may come to earth, as He has established it. There are upgrades in the Spirit that can only be accessed through God the Breaker.

When *breakthrough* happens, we don't want to stop there. We should press on to *breakout* of the old structures and *break forth* into the fullness of God's glory. What do you need *breakthrough* for? What do you need to *breakout* from? God wants you to *break forth* into His glorious realms of life and light, living in His delight.

Let us rejoice in all that God is doing and celebrate the One who is faithful and true! And for right now, until that time of completeness, we have three things to do that will lead us toward that consummation. We are to trust steadily in God, to hope unswervingly, and to love extravagantly. *"The greatest of these is love"* (1 Corinthians 13:13 NIV).

I believe in miracles
I believe in miracles
Here they come
From the Faithful One
He is moving every stone
Hindrances now be gone
The breaker goes before us
He breaks through for us
Moving us from and into
He is faithful and true

Watch and see
Receive and believe
Arise and sing
Praise to the King
Rejoice in God
Breakthrough's happening!

9

Releasing Revelation

in Intercession

PROVERBS 25:2 SAYS, *"It is the glory of God to conceal a matter, but the glory of kings is to search out a matter."* We are a royal priesthood. We are kings and priests! As kings, we must search out the mysteries of God and decree them into the atmosphere.

Often in my devotional time with the Lord I will hear something that He is releasing from heaven to earth. This same "hearing" also happens to me as I'm interceding during corporate worship and in other settings. At first I wasn't quite sure what to do with this revelatory information, but as I grew relationally with the Lord, asking, seeking, and knocking, I learned how to partner with what He was revealing to me. I believe He gives us revelation so that we can agree with Him, and from that place of agreement we are to pray into His revelations and release them – decree them.

Revelation is released from heaven on earth to accomplish the will of the Father. It comes to us in many forms. At times messenger angels bring us God's revelation. At other times we will literally hear it or see it, and often we will perceive it and simply "know" His revelation to us.

It is important that we study real revelation so as not to be deceived by the false. I have had encounters from both the realms of darkness and the Kingdom of Light. I believe that all revelation from God brings a message of hope. It can also bring a warning or speak of destiny, but all revelation shows us God's will. If the Lord allows us to see what the enemy is doing, it is because we are to seek Him [God] about His strategy to overcome the works of darkness.

It is wisdom to always seek the Lord before engaging in any battles with the enemy. Too many of us have been fighting an enemy who has revealed his dark deceptions to fool us into wrestling with him and chasing after him, to distract us from the real battle. If we seek the Lord, we will only fight the battles we are called to fight. And we'll win those battles triumphantly! God always wins!

As the Lord began to teach me how to pray into His revelation, I became comfortable asking Him questions. He taught me that most often we make mistakes with His revelation in how we interpret and apply it. At a conference once I saw a very large angel kneeling on the platform facing the people. He was holding something in his hand. I didn't know what it was, so I asked the Lord to tell me what the angel was doing. He told me that the angel was there to commission people into their calling, but He didn't instruct me to do anything except pray and agree, so I simply agreed with what the Lord allowed me to see.

Right after this, Patricia King, who was hosting the event, came to the front and said, "The Lord wants to commission some people today," and she began to call people out to prophesy and pray over them. The Lord allowed me to see what He was doing even though I myself was not the one publicly releasing. He was teaching me how to partner with Him. This was my "school" time and it was between me and the Lord. He didn't instruct me to tell anyone anything. My part was simply to agree with Him.

In hindsight I can see that if I had sought out Patricia King and shared this revelation with her, it could have been awkward and might have seemed a bit self-promoting. I didn't know any of the leaders there at the time and they didn't know me. Revelation is not given to us so that we can boast about how spiritual we are or how in tune with God we are. It is for the purpose of releasing the Father's heart and His desires from heaven into earth. At this particular conference someone else was chosen to release God's revelation, not me.

I've already shared in a previous chapter what happened when I was in an intercessory prayer gathering: The Lord spoke to me and told me to have everyone get on their knees and seek Him. I spoke this revelation out, and as we got on our knees I sensed His presence come into the room. He then instructed me to put out my hands, and as I did I felt a weighty substance come into the palms of my hands. When I asked the Lord what it was, He said, "This is the gift of faith; you are to release it here and in other places when I tell you."

Since that time I have seen this gift of faith move mountains and release miracles of divine healing, salvation, and financial blessing. Great breakthroughs for the Kingdom followed this revelation and impartation. God was showing me that obedience is the key that opens the doors and windows of revelation. If I didn't know how to recognize God's voice, I would miss out on some of the greatest journeys into the heart of God.

Jesus said that His sheep know His voice. To know His voice we must cultivate a listening ear. The book of James, chapter 4, tells us to humble ourselves, submit to God, resist the devil and he will flee from us. If we draw near to God, He will draw near to us. The Lord gave me a simple acrostic to help me remember how to hear and discern His voice.

H. E. A. R.

H umble yourself

E ndure – wait upon the Lord

A ttentively listen

R eceive from the Lord

Here are three simple steps that help us to hear God's voice and tune into what the Lord is revealing:

1. **Submit yourself to God.** Allow Him to have rule and ownership of your life. Ask Him to quiet your mind.

2. **Resist the devil.** The devil may try to deceive you, but when you submit to God and resist the devil, he has to leave.

3. **Expect God to answer.** When you ask Him a question, wait for Him to answer. Be like Samuel, who said, *"Speak, for your servant is listening"* (1 Samuel 3:10).

Discerning the Voice of God from Other Voices

As we learn how to handle revelation in intercession, it's important to be able to discern between our own voice, the voice of the world, the voice of the enemy, and God's voice. Our own voice can have a striving tone to it, as if we are trying to convince ourselves or someone else. It can also be self-seeking and self-pleasing. The voice of God will never have those characteristics. The voice of the world will come to us through others, our peers, the media, and through work.

Remember the story in 1 Kings, chapter 13, of the prophet of God who was deceived by another prophet. He listened to the voice of one of his peers and not to the voice of God. The voice of the enemy is deceptive and can make us feel anxious and fearful, unsettled, guilty, and ashamed. It will try to convince us to choose from the Tree of Knowledge of Good and Evil rather than from the Tree of Life.

In contrast to those voices, the voice of God always brings peace, focus, and clarity. Sometimes God takes us on a treasure hunt in order to discern what He is saying, because He wants us to dig deep into His Word and draw close to Him.

When we press in to Him with patience and perseverance, we will know His will.

Helpful Suggestions for Hearing God

Through our intimacy with the Lord we can develop a listening ear and open heart to Him. As we focus our thoughts and our hearts on Him, and present all of ourselves to Him, we will receive from the Lord.

> This book of the law shall not depart from your mouth, but you shall meditate on it day and night, so that you may be careful to do according to all that is written in it; for then you will make your way prosperous, and then you will have success.
>
> —Joshua 1:8

> One thing I have asked from the Lord, that I shall seek: that I may dwell in the house of the Lord all the days of my life, to behold the beauty of the Lord and to meditate in His temple.　　　—Psalm 27:4

> Finally, brethren, whatever is true, whatever is honorable, whatever is right, whatever is pure, whatever is lovely, whatever is of good repute, if there is any excellence and if anything worthy of praise, dwell on these things.　　　—Philippians 4:8

There are times when His fragrance comes into the atmosphere of a room to help us discern what He is doing. I have had my entire office fill with the fragrance of crushed grapes or new wine, inviting me to drink deeply of His life and be filled with the joy of His presence. In a public meeting I have smelled sweet incense as our worship took us into the presence of God.

In contrast to the fragrance of heaven are the putrid smells of the enemy. I have smelled the burning of hell, like reeking sulfur, as the enemy tried to keep someone bound who I was ministering deliverance to. One of my encounters with the dark side happened when the Lord was exposing witchcraft that was operating in a particular person.

At that point in time I was not accustomed to having manifestations of the enemy appear. I was walking my dog beside the river and as I came to a bend on the path I saw a wolf standing on the rocks in the river. The Holy Spirit spoke to me to pray in the Spirit and as I did, the wolf disappeared. A short time later I was at the home of my mentor. After our time of sharing and prayer, she opened the front door to let me out and there across the street was the same wolf. We prayed and it left.

However, the wolf reappeared one Sunday morning at church on the children's empty playground. Again the Lord had me pray, and as I did He began to show me that there was a wolf in sheep's clothing in the church. He had me come and stand behind a person who was praying over others at the altar. The Lord clearly revealed to me the assignment of the enemy through this person was to sow division and discord, tearing apart families. The Lord had me begin to pray for this person to repent or to leave. I went to the leadership of the church but they were unfamiliar with this kind of rev-elation and warned me to not be too zealous.

I stayed humble and submitted and sought the Lord even more because I could see the danger. Soon afterward, that person left the church. When that person returned one Sun-day, I met them at the entrance, took their hand and released the dunamis power of the Holy Spirit. They left, and this time they didn't return.

I learned a lot from this encounter. I knew that I needed God to reveal what was going on. He showed me that the enemy fears those who see, discern, hear, and receive revela-tion. I was able to see firsthand how the enemy tries to infil-trate the ranks of God's church, and that we need humble, discerning, loving watchmen who will partner with God to protect His people. This learning process was progressive and required me to spend a great deal of time before the Lord seeking His revelation. I was fortunate to have a mature men-tor who walked through this with me and helped me to dis-cern and trust God.

Hearing God is vital in this hour. We need to hear clearly so that Holy Spirit can release His gifts to us and the Lord's light can shine through us.

> Whether it is pleasant or unpleasant, we will listen to the voice of the Lord our God to whom we are send-ing you, so that it may go well with us when we listen to voice of the Lord our God.
>
> —Jeremiah 42:6

Hearing God is vital in this hour. We need to hear clearly so that Holy Spirit can release His gifts to us and the Lord's light can shine through us.

As we grow in our relationship with the Lord and He fine-tunes our hearing through sweet fellowship with Holy Spirit, I believe He will release greater things for us to do so that we might bring glory to the Father. But first, we must know Him. We must enter by the blood of the Lamb into the Holy of Holies. There is no other way to come into His presence. If we will apply the blood of the Lamb and come boldly into His throne room of grace, He will have much to say to us.

Jesus promised us that we would do greater works than He did during His time on earth, and I truly believe He meant it. We must hear what the Spirit is saying so we can fulfill God's purpose for this hour, to be released into the wonderful destiny He has for us.

If we are going to walk with the living Word in us, we need to be motivated by His love. Everything the Lord does comes from His love in the power of His Holy Spirit. We love Him by loving others. We need to allow His love to fill us so that it overflows from us to others. When we have the living Word of God in us in the power of His Spirit, we can "walk" with Him. How awesome to walk with the living Word of God!

Now, beloved, please understand that prophecy should only come from a heart of love. The Holy Spirit loves to be where love is. His voice breathes life and love!

> If I have the gift of prophecy and can fathom all mysteries and all knowledge, and if I have a faith that can move mountains, but do not have love, I am nothing. —1 Corinthians 13:2 NIV

Getting to know the Lord and learning to hear His voice is like going on an exciting treasure hunt! He wants us to seek Him, for He is the pearl of greatest value. He speaks to us in many ways, and it's important to let Him choose the way. To hear Him, you must know Him, and to know Him you must spend time with Him. Worship Him, read His Word, be quiet before Him, ask, seek, and knock.

Some people are afraid of the supernatural aspect of God and yet they forget that God is the only One who creates. Satan can only counterfeit what is real. People who counterfeit money are so good that an untrained eye can't tell the difference. Do you know that you have to study real money so you can tell the difference between the real and the fake? We have to *know* God so we won't be deceived by the fakes.

Don't be afraid to ask for His gifts. Don't be afraid to discover God's voice. As long as you are searching for Him with a clean heart, He will keep you from being deceived. There was a time when I was deceived by a nice sounding lie that said, "Seek only the Giver and not the gift." I used to believe that lie until God showed me the deception in it.

We need *all* that God has prepared for us, because Satan doesn't always come in an evil-looking package. He can come as an angel of light in a good-looking package. We need to seek God and ask of Him, and He will give us the revelation of *His* truth. God loves us and wants to be closer to us. He wants to give us beautiful packages of His love, His grace, and His mercy. He wants to give us His gifts and He wants us to grow in the fruit of His Spirit so that the gifts will be good for others, also.

I want to share with you a very important revelation God gave me several years ago about prayer. It's profound in its simplicity, and it's for everyone who prays. The Lord woke me one morning at 4:11 a.m. and proceeded to remind me that 411 is the number we use to call Information, while 911 is what we use in emergencies. Then He showed me why there is a distinct difference between a 911 prayer and a 411 prayer.

Notice that I am putting 911 before 411. How many of us tend to do that in our prayer lives, calling up the Lord when we have an emergency instead of constantly "talking" to Him to receive His information. If we lived praying 411 prayers, connecting to the operator of our faith and seeking His information, think how we would live in His wisdom, knowing His offensive strategies, instead of always living on the defensive!

We have been given a direct line to the Lord, and I believe He desires that we get to the place of divine communication with Him, where we are asking, seeking, knocking, and waiting to hear what He has to say. Mark, chapter 4, says:

> He told them, "The secret of the kingdom of God has been given to you. But to those on the outside everything is said in parables."   —Mark 4:11 NIV

We have been given the keys to the Kingdom! By His Spirit He gives us understanding of the revelation (information) He is imparting to us. We are permitted to understand the secret.

His Word is full of invitations to come and ask for what we need.

> But if any of you lacks wisdom, let him ask of God, who gives to all generously and without reproach, and it will be given to him. —James 1:5

When we call to Him, He can't wait to hear our voice. Listen to what the Bridegroom says to His bride in Song of Solomon:

> O my dove, in the clefts of the rock, in the secret place of the steep pathway. Let me see your form, let me hear your voice; for your voice is sweet, and your form is lovely. —Song of Solomon 2:14

Our voice and our words are sweet to the Lord. He longs to hear our voice. When we hear the voice of one we love in the midst of a crowd, we will turn and look for that one. That is how it is for us with our Beloved. His eyes are always looking for those who love Him and whose hearts are completely His. We are invited into a living relationship with Him, where prayers are not just requests but the place where we receive Him and His love.

10

Interceding from Heaven to Earth

WHEN JESUS' DISCIPLES asked Him to teach them how to pray, He responded, "Pray, then, in this way":

"Our Father who art in Heaven, hallowed be Thy name. Thy Kingdom come. Thy will be done on earth, as it is in Heaven. Give us this day our daily bread. And forgive us our debts, as we forgive our debtors. And lead us not into temptation, but deliver us from evil. For Thine is the Kingdom, and the power and the glory for ever. Amen."

—Matthew 6:9-13 KJ21

In this, the Lord's Prayer, Jesus is giving us keys to unlock access to His revelation. He's opening up the storehouses of heaven, the mysteries of heaven. He is teaching us how to intercede from heaven to earth. This is not a complicated model for prayer. If we come at it with a childlike faith, we can learn to intercede this way.

In Ephesians, Paul gives us a revelation about intercession.

But because of his great love for us, God, who is rich in mercy, made us alive with Christ even when we were dead in transgressions—it is by grace you have been saved. And God raised us up with Christ and seated us with him in the heavenly realms in Christ Jesus, in order that in the coming ages he might show the incomparable riches of his grace, expressed in his kindness to us in Christ Jesus.

—Ephesians 2:4-7 NIV

What a glorious, heavenly perspective! Our view in life should be from just such a heavenly perspective. We have been made alive in Christ, seated with Him in heavenly places, and we receive His view and His perspective because we have His mind. And if we have the mind of Christ, we should be releasing heaven's goodness on earth through our intercession.

Sometimes our view of intercession can be too limited. Intercession is not only an act of prayer. As intercessors, we are advocates and ambassadors of heaven, and we are to fight – whether it is for individuals, churches, schools, the workplace, cities, regions, or nations – we are to fight for those who are bound by dark clouds of deception, and then release the light of truth to them – God's truth as revealed in Christ Jesus.

There are so many marvelous ways to release His truths. We can do this in prayer, in works of art, in poetry, songs, theatrical productions, dance, prophetic ministry, and even such unlikely venues as a business meeting.

The goal is to break out of our church boxes and break open the walls of the church. When we do this, we discover that as intercessors we are to be like Jesus the great Intercessor, and be advocates and ambassadors of His Kingdom of light.

As an advocate of heaven, Jesus only did what He saw the Father doing.

> Therefore Jesus answered and was saying to them, "Truly, truly, I say to you, the Son can do nothing of Himself, unless it is something He sees the Father doing; for whatever the Father does, these things the Son also does in like manner. For the Father loves the Son, and shows Him all things that He Himself is doing; and the Father will show Him greater works than these, so that you will marvel."
>
> —John 5:19-20

Jesus knew that He was loved, and He followed His Father's leading out of this love relationship. We too can embrace the revelation of this love relationship as we intercede using the Lord's Prayer.

"Our Father who art in Heaven, hallowed be Thy
name. Thy kingdom come. Thy will be done on earth,
as it is in Heaven."   —Matthew 6:9-10 KJ21

When we worship the Creator of the Universe, giving
honor and glory to the Father, He draws near to us. His eyes
literally turn toward us! Our intimate gaze through worship
and adoration causes Him to look at us and see into us, and
we're forever changed. As we behold Him, we become like
Him and He flows out of our hearts. This transformation in
worship aligns our hearts with His heart and we see the world
from His perspective.

In the Lord's Prayer, we see a declaration of adoration and
honor to the Father. If we press in to this place of focused
worship, magnifying God's magnificent name and proclaim-
ing His goodness, we become His living advocates. We enter
through the gates of heaven into His courts of praise through
thanksgiving! As we approach His throne of grace, He will
give us eyes to see and ears to hear His fresh revelations. The
cares of the world will begin to slip away and love will swell
like a crashing wave against the shores of our heart.

As this marvelous love washes over us, we become soft in
His presence, with the essence of Him permeating every fiber
of our being. The atmosphere of the Kingdom of heaven invades our earthly realm. We no longer fellowship from lists
and agendas. Now we enter into the chambers of His heart to
beat with the very rhythms of heaven!

Pure spiritual life flows from His heart into our hearts. In this intimate place He releases His revelation. Sometimes it is in the form of text from Scripture, sometimes as pictures or visions, or words and insight. As we rest in this place and listen, we can see and receive what the Father is releasing to us. And as His revelations unfold, we can begin to agree and decree what He is revealing. The prophet Isaiah called this the "tongue of disciples."

> The Lord God has given Me the tongue of disciples, that I may know how to sustain the weary one with a word. He awakens Me morning by morning, He awakens my ear to listen as a disciple. The Lord God has opened My ear; and I was not disobedient nor did I turn back.   —Isaiah 50:4-5

The Lord will give us the words to speak. He will tell us what to pray, what to declare and decree, what will bring refreshing and life. All this comes out of our intimate times with Him. It is in this posture, before Him, that He wakes our ears. In His presence we are fine-tuned to hear, to see, and to release what He shows us. In this intimate place, tenacious courage to obey Him is infused into us! In His presence the very essence of His being empowers us, and we are able to trust and obey Him.

> You will make known to me the path of life; in Your presence is fullness of joy; in Your right hand there are pleasures forever.   —Psalm 16:11

"Give us this day our daily bread."

—Matthew 6:11 KJ21

To do the work of intercession we need bread, and the bread we need is Jesus, the Bread of Life. Our abiding in Him unlocks all our prayers and intercession.

> Jesus then said to them, "Truly, truly, I say to you, it is not Moses who has given you the bread out of heaven, but it is My Father who gives you the true bread out of heaven. For the bread of God is that which comes down out of heaven, and gives life to the world." Then they said to Him, "Lord, always give us this bread." Jesus said to them, "I am the bread of life; he who comes to Me will not hunger, and he who believes in Me will never thirst."
>
> —John 6:32-35

When we receive Jesus, we live in an abiding that brings us into the revealed will of the Father. To abide in Christ is to live in a faith that believes and receives what the Father has already established He wants to do. Prayers and acts of intercession that come from the Father's will begin to happen because He has been looking for our agreement with Him. John 15:7 says:

> If you abide in Me, and My words abide in you, ask whatever you wish, and it will be done for you.

Answered prayers and intercession come from our abiding. To abide is to live and dwell fully in Him. Jesus has made a way for us to live an abundant life of fulfilled hopes and dreams. We need only to believe and receive. In Exodus, the Lord commanded Moses to set the bread of His presence on the table, where it was to remain before the Lord at all times. That was under the old covenant.

Jesus, the new covenant, is the bread of life that brings us into the presence of the Father. His blood has given us access to the Father. We can come freely and boldly into the throne room of grace because of Jesus! It is His good pleasure to give to us.

When we find ourselves in a place of need, it could be that we have not asked the Father from our aligned place of abiding in Christ. An aligned heart abiding in His presence can ask from a pure place; and the pure in heart will see God.

"And forgive us our debts, as we forgive our debtors."   —Matthew 6:12 KJ21

One of the ways in which we can partner with Christ is to release debts. When we release a debt, we take that which is due us and we let it go, give it up, send it away. In other words, we forgive.

As we sit in the presence of the Lord, we are to release ourselves, to release others, and to release the issues we are praying into from all debts. We literally stand in our place in Christ and forgive the debts of others, of cities, of generations. As we do this we partner with Christ in His Kingdom purposes for today.

Jesus appears after His resurrection to His disciples many times. In John 20, Jesus appeared and said this to His disciples:

> "Peace be with you; as the Father has sent Me, I also send you." And when He had said this, He breathed on them and said to them, "Receive the Holy Spirit. If you forgive the sins of any, their sins have been forgiven them; if you retain the sins of any, they have been retained." —John 20:21-23

As I read this passage, I am undone by the revelation of the Father through Jesus. He releases peace to His disciples and then tells them that as the Father sent Him, so He sends them. He then breathes on them and tells them to receive the Holy Spirit, commissioning them into the ministry of intercession in forgiveness of sins! We, too, share in this commission!

At the cross, Jesus made perfect intercession for all who draw near and receive the life offered through this new and perfect covenant. We get to be those who are advocates like Him through our acts of intercession, to bring others into wholeness and fullness in Him.

In Hebrews we read of Jesus' role as "The Intercessor" who has brought us into this new covenant:

> And inasmuch as it was not without an oath (for they indeed became priests without an oath, but He with an oath through the One who said to Him, "The

At the cross, Jesus made perfect intercession for all who draw near and receive the life offered through this new and perfect covenant. We get to be those who are advocates like Him through our acts of intercession.

Lord has sworn and will not change His mind, 'You are a priest forever'"); so much the more also Jesus has become the guarantee of a better covenant. The former priests, on the one hand, existed in greater numbers because they were prevented by death from continuing, but Jesus, on the other hand, because He continues forever, holds His priesthood permanently. Therefore He is able also to save forever those who draw near to God through Him, since He always lives to make intercession for them.

For it was fitting for us to have such a high priest, holy, innocent, undefiled, separated from sinners and exalted above the heavens; who does not need daily, like those high priests, to offer up sacrifices, first for His own sins and then for the sins of the people, because this He did once for all when He offered up Himself. For the Law appoints men as high priests who are weak, but the word of the oath, which came after the Law, appoints a Son, made perfect forever.

—Hebrews 7:20-28

Jesus, the perfect sacrifice, has made a way for us forever. As we step into His life, abiding in the finished work of the cross, all that He has, all the fullness that is in Him is available to us who believe. As we release debts, we are brought into the blessing of the new covenant, called to live in a new way.

> Therefore, brethren, since we have confidence to enter the holy place by the blood of Jesus, by a new and living way which He inaugurated for us through the veil, that is, His flesh, and since we have a great priest over the house of God, let us draw near with a sincere heart in full assurance of faith, having our hearts sprinkled clean from an evil conscience and our bodies washed with pure water. Let us hold fast the confession of our hope without wavering, for He who promised is faithful; and let us consider how to stimulate one another to love and good deeds.
> —Hebrews 10:19-24

We can take hold of this bold courage to be steadfast and enter into the presence of God through the blood of Jesus, gaining access from our place in the Father's house. Everything in His Kingdom is available for us to partner with Him in seeing Jesus, the Lamb of God, receive His full reward for His suffering. This is the cry of the ages!

> Therefore repent and return, so that your sins may be wiped away, in order that times of refreshing may come from the presence of the Lord.   —Acts 3:19

True repentance brings us into the presence of the Lord where He washes us clean from all sin. Then He releases a shower of His presence that refreshes us from all the dredges that trap us, the sins and snares that try to attach to us. I like to pray Psalm 51 as a prayer of repentance. I find this psalm to be like a spiritual cleansing pad that will reveal sins that may be hidden from my sight.

> "And lead us not into temptation, but deliver us from evil."   —Matthew 6:13 KJ21

It is wisdom to pray for God's protection from the evil one and to cry out that we would not fall into temptation.

> So, if you think you are standing firm, be careful that you don't fall! No temptation has overtaken you except what is common to mankind. And God is faithful; he will not let you be tempted beyond what you can bear. But when you are tempted, he will also provide a way out so that you can endure it.
> —1 Corinthians 10:12-13 NIV

God knows that the enemy is releasing snares and temptations, trying to turn our hearts away from Him. Sometimes the temptation is to get us to believe lies about who God is so that we will accuse God and become angry with Him. In the Garden, Satan fed Adam and Eve a lie, telling them that God had been withholding from them those things that would empower them. Because they believed Satan's lie, that lie separated them from the power of life that had enabled them to live in all the fullness of what God had for them.

Thank God in Jesus that what was lost in the fall of man in the Garden was restored when Jesus chose not His own will, but the Father's will in another garden. Jesus plucked our feet out of the net. He knows that the enemy is setting up snares to trap us and trip us up, but He will deliver us when we trust Him.

We are to remember that the Lord pardons *all* our iniquity. He delivers us from *every* snare. He leads us in His way and wants our soul to prosper! He will pluck our feet out of every net, every trap and every snare. If we can remember this, we can stop beating ourselves up when we get trapped, and instead call on the Lord who delivers us! God is our Strong Deliverer!

> Surely he will save you from the fowler's snare and from the deadly pestilence.   —Psalm 91:3 NIV

> I call upon the Lord, who is worthy to be praised, and I am saved from my enemies.   —Psalm 18:3

> "For thine is the kingdom, and the power, and the glory, for ever. Amen."   —Matthew 6:13 KJ21

The Lord's Prayer ends in the same way that it began – in worship, with praise and adoration of the One who sits upon the throne!

Here is one way I pray the Lord's Prayer. I use it not as a formula, but as a springboard to bring me into greater depths of prayer and intercession.

Our glorious Father, awesome in power and holy above all others; wonderful, magnificent, and hallowed is Your Name! You are all together worthy of all my praise and adoration! I thank You for filling me with Your life, hope, grace, and power! I lift up my eyes to you and call upon your precious Name. You are seated in the heavenlies, filled with all wisdom, knowledge, and understanding. I worship You, love You and adore You.

Let Your Kingdom of righteousness, peace, joy, truth, life and light be released into this situation I am praying for. Open my eyes to see from Your heavenly perspective how this can be reconciled on earth to manifest Your Kingdom. I submit to You in every place and draw near to You. Thank You for revealing Your will to me, as Your Word says that I will be filled with the knowledge of Your will in all spiritual wisdom and understanding so that I will walk in a manner worthy of the Lord to please You in all respects, bearing fruit in every good work, and increasing in the knowledge of God strengthened with all power, according to Your glorious might, for the attaining of steadfastness and patience ... I joyfully give thanks to You, Father, for releasing the inheritance of Your Kingdom of Light.

Father, thank You for sending Your Son Jesus, the living Bread of Life, from heaven. I ask for the Bread of Life to be made fully manifest in every realm of life. Thank You for releasing the bread of Your presence. Thank You for the bread of provision for every need. Your bread sustains me, fills me, heals me and gives me life. I rejoice to abide in You, Jesus Christ, my friend and companion who will never leave but daily loads me with the benefits of heaven.

Father, forgive me (and those I am praying for) all our debts. Release us from all sin, from every place of robbing, every debt, curse, hex, vex, and word that has kept us bound in a prison of lack. I loose myself from all debt. I choose to repent and change my thinking to line up with the mind of Christ and Your heart. Thank You for delivering me from every iniquity that has bound me in the dark places. I choose to forgive those who have sinned against me. I release them from every debt.

Father, deliver me from all evil. Pluck my feet from the fowler's snare and set me on the path of Life and Light. Keep me from all temptation that would steal me away from You. Teach me truth, and help me to guard my heart with all diligence so that I may fully walk in Your ways.

To You I lift up all glory, honor ,and praise! Yours is the Kingdom of blessing and Your dominion is holy into all eternity as You reign in all the earth and heavens. I worship and honor You with all my life. Amen."

11

Rivers of Living Water

ONE OF THE MOST POWERFUL, transforming revelations I have ever received from the Lord has to do with how we keep the enemy out of our lives, our churches, our cities, and our regions. This revelation came from a simple question stirred up in me as I was watching a well-known healing evangelist interviewing a minister on his daily program. They were discussing from Luke 11:

> When the unclean spirit goes out of a man, it passes through waterless places seeking rest, and not finding any, it says, "I will return to my house from which I came." And when it comes, it finds it swept and put in order. Then it goes and takes along seven other spirits more evil than itself, and they go in and live there; and the last state of that man becomes worse than the first. —Luke 11:24-26

One of the men asked, "Why is it that the evil spirit can come back?" I was prompted in my spirit to ask the same question, and as I did the Lord began to speak to me His revelation about living water and the river of God. This chapter is about the revelation the Lord taught me from His Word and how important it is to keep the river flowing purely in our own lives and the life of the church. As the Lord began to teach me, He took me to Zechariah:

> Rejoice greatly, Daughter Zion! Shout, Daughter Jerusalem! See, your king comes to you, righteous and victorious, lowly and riding on a donkey, on a colt, the foal of a donkey. I will take away the chariots from Ephraim and the warhorses from Jerusalem, and the battle bow will be broken. He will proclaim peace to the nations. His rule will extend from sea to sea and from the River to the ends of the earth.

> As for you, because of the blood of my covenant with you, I will free your prisoners from the waterless pit. Return to your fortress, you prisoners of hope; even now I announce that I will restore twice as much to you.   —Zechariah 9:9-12 NIV

This prophesy about Jesus gave me a key that transformed the way I think and pray. Verse 11 says that because of the blood of God's covenant with us, He has set us free from the waterless pit. Jesus poured out His blood and God made a new covenant with us, and everything we need is in the blood covenant.

In the same way, after the supper he took the cup, saying, "This cup is the new covenant in my blood, which is poured out for you."   —Luke 22:20 NIV

Because of the blood of His covenant, He delivers us from the waterless pit. Luke 11, verse 24, tells us that the evil spirit departed, passing through waterless places seeking rest. It was looking for a waterless pit because the enemy cannot be in God's living water. When the Lord's side was pierced on the cross, blood and water poured out. This was His life poured out to set us free from every waterless place. The blood of Jesus has made a way for us to come into the presence of God.

In God's presence we are made new. We are restored. We receive life. From the overflow of Himself, Jesus fills us, and we in turn release that life, that river of living water, out into the world. Psalm 16 says,

You will make known to me the path of life; in Your presence is fullness of joy; in Your right hand there are pleasures forever.   —Psalm 16:11

When we look at the story of the Samaritan woman in John, chapter 4, we see a woman encountering the One who could deliver her from the waterless pit and fill her with life.

The word for *living* that Jesus uses here is *Zao*, which means "to live and breathe and be among the living; to enjoy a real and true life, active and blessed; a life having a vital power in and of itself and exerting that same power upon the soul."[3] WOW! Look at what the living water will do when it flows in our lives. It will bless us and give us strength, energy and power. We will enjoy *real* life.

In John 4, verse 28 we see that she left her waterpot, the vessel that she filled with earthly water. It became unimportant in light of the revelation of the living water that she had been given to drink. She had received living water that set her free from all fear.

A woman scorned became an evangelist filled with vigor, life, strength, and vital power, fully alive in Christ. Many believed and a city was transformed because the One who gives living water came to seek and save those who are rejected, forgotten, scorned, and lost. He came for us all.

Jesus speaks to the people again about this living water:

On the last and greatest day of the festival, Jesus stood and said in a loud voice, "Let anyone who is thirsty come to me and drink. Whoever believes in me, as Scripture has said, rivers of living water will flow from within them." By this he meant the Spirit, whom those who believed in him were later to receive. Up to that time the Spirit had not been given, since Jesus had not yet been glorified.

—John 7:37-39 NIV

---

[3] Blue Letter Bible. "Dictionary and Word Search for Zao (Strong's 2198)." Blue Letter Bible. 1996-2012. 4 Oct 2012. http://www.blueletterbible.org/lang/lexicon/lexicon.cfm?strongs=G2198

My response to this passage is, "Give me a drink, Lord! I thirst for You, for Your living water!"

How do we as intercessors stay hydrated and drink of this living water? Let me begin by saying that it is not legal for a Christian to be dry! We may go through the desert, but we have living water available from the Lord. We just need to come to Him and drink. I want to jump into the fountain of God's life and His goodness! He is light, and this light is full of life and delight. Oh, to pray, to stand, to come into agreement with the God who gives us drink from His river of delights! Psalm 46 tells us that:

> There is a river whose streams make glad the city of God, the holy place where the Most High dwells.
> —Psalm 46:4 NIV

When God's river flows in us and through us, we release the life we carry. There can be no dry places in us – no dry spots for the enemy to land in. Even in the wilderness, the Lord will open up a river to drink from.

> He opened the rock, and water gushed out; it flowed like a river in the desert. For he remembered his holy promise given to his servant Abraham. He brought out his people with rejoicing, his chosen ones with shouts of joy. —Psalm 105:41-43 NIV

> He turned the desert into pools of water and the parched ground into flowing springs; there he brought the hungry to live, and they founded a city where they

could settle. They sowed fields and planted vineyards that yielded a fruitful harvest; he blessed them, and their numbers greatly increased, and he did not let their herds diminish.

—Psalm 107:35-38 NIV

Why does the enemy use good people to come against the movement of the river of God? Because he knows only that which has life can live where the river of God flows. The enemy can't dwell in the river. When we see demonic manifestations, it is often because the enemy has encountered the river of God and is being exposed. He will try to counterattack the exposure by bringing criticism to people's hearts in the form of lies that pollute, plug up, and stop the flow of God's living water.

We are called to be as wise as serpents and as gentle as doves to discern what is truth and what is a lie. But even when we are living in the light of God's truth, the enemy continues to prowl, doing everything to shut down the move of God and stop the river from flowing. I saw this happen.

In 2004, we were part of a crusade in which we saw incredible breakthroughs in salvations, healings, and deliverance. The meetings were glorious. The presence of the Lord was tangible and weighty. The stadium where we were meeting filled every night with people rushing to the altar. It was a monumental crusade.

The next year, 2005, when we came back to the same city, I was struck with the darkness and lack of passion among the same churches that had gone passionately after God the year before. The meetings were not well attended and the warfare was intense. Even in our briefing with the team I could hear the lies of the enemy being released.

I spoke out the Word of the Lord – to guard ourselves, seek His face, and guard the unity among the team. But many on the team became critical of each other, and the lack of unity opened the doors to even more darkness. Some of the leaders had fallen into adultery in the year since our last crusade. They were not coming together as they had before. I was distraught and cried out to the Lord in my room. I got on my face before Him, seeking His heart.

The Father revealed to me that in 2004, as we interceded for the crusade, we were successful in kicking the powers and principalities out of the region, but we failed to partner with the churches ensuring that the replacement from God's Kingdom would continue to the gap. Instead we released the river, but the unity was not in place to hold the ground. The enemy came back into that dry hole with more wicked rulers than had been there in the first place.

I was beside myself with grief over the mistake we had made. Even though I was not the one who had gone into this warfare over principalities, I was the leader and I hadn't stopped it. It was after this trip that the revelation of rivers of living waters came to me.

Beloved, if we are going to get demonic powers and principalities to depart a region, we must have unity between the intercessory team and the leaders so that the necessary follow-up can take place. If the leaders in the region don't know how to hold the ground that has been overcome, the enemy will come back like a thief in the night to kill, steal, and destroy.

From this teachable season with the Lord, I learned that when I am on a short mission trip, my assignment is to release heaven; to let the river of God flow and bring life. And unless I am building relationships with the leaders, I am not to go in and displace demonic rulers. I can bind them and forbid them to operate in our gatherings, but when I'm gone others may not know how to keep them from coming back.

It is a better strategy to seek the Lord as to how to release His Kingdom, seeking the strategy of the Lord each and every time we intercede. What we do in one city may not be what the Lord wants to do in another. Sometimes it is, but we won't know if we don't inquire of the Lord.

Jesus taught us to pray to the Father for His Kingdom to come and His will to be done. When we do this, all of heaven is available. He sends the angels, the resources, the wisdom, and the understanding to partner with Him.

When I am walking in a relationship of grace and humility, and am able to sit down with the leaders and intercessors before a crusade or a conference or a meeting, then I can strategize with them. We are called to occupy by releasing the Kingdom, but we must have a strategy and a plan. No army should go into a region without a strategy and a plan to occupy.

Too many times, when leaders and intercessors do not communicate, all kinds of trouble can develop and stop the river of God from flowing. When we sit down with one another in grace and humility and communicate, we open the door for God's strategy to be revealed to us.

I can still hear the voice of a precious leader sharing with me that, yes, he was seeing my strategy, but my strategy was future-forward and it was his job to steer the ship slowly into new waters so as not to wreck it. I got it; I understood and we were able to partner together to see God come in glorious ways.

Relationships that stay centered in the heart of God and His Kingdom always bring great freedom for God's river to flow and for His life to fill the church.

As intercessors we are not to drink from polluted rivers or other cisterns!

For My people have committed two evils: they have forsaken Me, the fountain of living waters, to hew for themselves cisterns, broken cisterns that can hold no water.   —Jeremiah 2:13

Jeremiah 2, verse 18, says that they were drinking from other rivers, and the rest of that chapter goes on to share how the people refused to follow the Lord and chose instead idolatry and sin. Beloved, be careful who you listen to, what you agree with. We are to listen only to the voice of the Shepherd, not to the voice of criticism, which is religion and fear.

Recently, on two different ministry trips on two different continents, the Lord directed us to go to the riverhead and take back the river of the city. I had never done this before. We went in obedience, with bread, wine, and oil, engaging in repentance. Led by the Holy Spirit, we tossed pieces of bread into the river just as it is done in the ancient Jewish practice of Tashlich, which is a ritual observed by many Jews during Rosh Hashanah.

In Hebrew, *Tashlich* means "casting off" and involves symbolically casting off one's sins from the previous year by tossing pieces of bread or food into a river of flowing water, symbolically washing our sins away, just as the river carries the pieces of bread away. In this manner, we can start the New Year with a clean slate, a short list with God.

After we had cast our bread into the water, we took communion. Then we staked Scriptures at the bank of the river, pouring wine and oil over each of them as the apostolic leader in the group led us in prayer, declaring the river the Lord's. The prophet Micah says,

> You will again have compassion on us; you will tread our sins underfoot and hurl all our iniquities into the depths of the sea.   —Micah 7:19 NIV

How do we keep get the river flowing? The river of God is the manifest presence of God, when His glory comes and fills people and places. Ruth Ward-Heflin understood how to stand in the river of God. A Christian minister both in the U.S. and abroad, she had great impact for the Kingdom, flowing in the glory of the Lord, leading people in times of thanksgiving and high praise. Her worshipful adoration would bring the Lord's glory into a place and then the Lord would begin to move as He chose, in the midst of His glory.

Moses and Solomon built the temple of the Lord according to God's plans, and the glory of the Lord dwelt there. We, too, have been made according the Lord's design. When we yield our lives to Him we become His dwelling place. His presence is *in* us, but He also wants to *surround* us with His manifest presence. He is continually filling His houses [us] with His glory!

On one of Global Awakening's Youth Power Invasion trips, we experienced the glory of the Lord fill our meeting. I was in the intercession room with a handful of youth. We were crying out to the Lord, worshipping and adoring Him. Our focus was that He would show us His glory. The speaker, Jason Westerfield, requested that I come out and join him on the platform. Together we began to release words of knowledge. As people stepped forward in response to the words of knowledge, they were instantly healed. Miracles happened all over the room. The manifest glorious presence of God was among us to heal, save, and deliver. The river of life was flowing freely!

When we wait in the Lord's presence in prayer and worship, listening and receiving all that He has for us, He will saturate us with His river of life. Some streams in the body of Christ call this soaking. I don't know if what the Holy Spirit had taught me to do has any kind of name. I just know that

He has brought me into His resting place with worship, instrumental songs and reflective songs that focus me on Him.

In this place of intense focus on Him, without any agenda but simply resting in worship and adoration, He gives me more than I could ever imagine. When I come out of these soaking times, I leak the essence of His presence. He permeates my entire being.

We can all be people of His presence, filled with the essence of His glory. His essence is the substance, the fragrance and the matter of God. When we are saturated in the essence of His presence, we have His divine nature filling us. It is the living water promised to us. There are no more dry places, no more access for the enemy, when we let the river flow. Many of us have had visitations, but, oh, how we should long for His habitation in our lives.

When the disciples were waiting for the promise of the Father in the Upper Room after Jesus had ascended, they were in one accord, praying and worshipping. As they waited in unity, praying and worshipping God, the river of the Holy Spirit came and filled them. Tongues of fire came upon them and they were given boldness, courage, anointing, wisdom, and understanding – the fullness of Christ promised. They were filled with the essence of God.

God's essence is who He is and what He does. He is Creator, lover, glorious restorer, loving-kindness, joy, peace, righteousness, hope, faith, life, light, radiant beauty, healer, provider, and so much more!

12

A Holy Renaissance:
A Lovelution

I BELIEVE GOD IS CALLING US as intercessors to be part of His Love Revolution, His renaissance of creative believers empowered with His heart. I see a remnant of holy radical ones who are coming out of hiddenness, rejection, and betrayal to become part of what God is doing in this hour. Together, we are His Lovelutionaries, releasing recovery to those who have been robbed, blinded, deceived, and lost, as we awaken humanity to the truth of God's great love and supernatural grace powers.

God's fearless heart of love goes into all the earth to seek and find that which has been snatched by the enemy or has wandered away. The sound of heaven is stirring in hearts, causing us to come into a calibration of oneness with the heart of the Father. It is truly glorious!

Intrepid warriors come from every walk of life: students, business people, artisans, teachers, painters, mathematicians, scientists, singers, musicians, and the list goes on. They are fearless, loving, kind, and tenacious. They are happy intercessors who release the strength of joy! They will not give up or back down. They are marked by heaven and sealed in the fire of God's love. They are friends of Jesus and they love His friends. They are generous and willing to lay down their lives.

Intrepid warriors are history makers and, even if no one on earth ever knows them by name, they are known in heaven. They live in love and light, and the light in them chases darkness away and releases hope. They are part of the Mission Possible team that believes with God all things are possible. They are hope reformers, faith releasers, and love igniters. They are passionate and faithful, holy and forgiven.

Intrepid warriors know that God is for them and no one can stand against them, and they bear the love standard of the Glad King. They are the bride of Christ, the sons of God, the ones written in the Lamb's book. They are loved by God. The characteristics of intrepid warriors are found in His Word.

As you read the following Scriptures, it is my prayer that your heart will be stirred to *fearless* intercession and you, too, will become an intrepid warrior.

The Word of God establishes itself in the heart of God's intrepid ones.

Do not be overcome by evil, but overcome evil with good.   —Romans 12:21 NIV

You are from God, little children, and have overcome them; because greater is He who is in you than he who is in the world.　　　　　　　−1 John 4:4

For whatever is born of God overcomes the world; and this is the victory that has overcome the world − our faith.　　　　　　　−1 John 5:4

The Word abides in Lovelutionaries, overcoming the evil one.

I am writing to you, fathers, because you know Him who has been from the beginning. I am writing to you, young men, because you have overcome the evil one. I have written to you, children, because you know the Father. I have written to you, fathers, because you know Him who has been from the beginning. I have written to you, young men, because you are strong, and the word of God abides in you, and you have overcome the evil one.

　　　　　　　−1 John 2:13-14

These will wage war against the Lamb, and the Lamb will overcome them, because He is Lord of lords and King of kings, and those who are with Him are the called and chosen and faithful.

　　　　　　　−Revelation 17:14

We Are the Bride of Christ.

And I saw the holy city, new Jerusalem, coming down out of heaven from God, made ready as a bride adorned for her husband. —Revelation 21:2

Let us rejoice and be glad and give the glory to Him, for the marriage of the Lamb has come and His bride has made herself ready. —Revelation 19:7

Great grace is poured out upon us as we humble ourselves before the Lord.

But He gives a greater grace. Therefore it says, "God is opposed to the proud, but gives grace to the humble."
—James 4:6

He had told you, O man, what is good; and what does the Lord require of you but to do justice, to love kindness, and to walk humbly with your God.
—Micah 6:8

We seek the Lord first in all things, and keep our eyes fixed on Him.

Therefore if you have been raised up with Christ, keep seeking the things above, where Christ is, seated at the right hand of God. —Colossians 3:1

But from there you will seek the Lord your God, and you will find Him if you search for Him with all your heart and all your soul. —Deuteronomy 4:29

As we pursue God's Kingdom and His purposes first, we choose the Lord's will and not our own.

> "Your kingdom come. Your will be done, on earth as it is in heaven." —Matthew 6:10

> And this, not as we had expected, but they first gave themselves to the Lord and to us by the will of God.
> —2 Corinthians 8:5

We recognize our need of a Savior and fall upon the Lord Jesus.

> For all have sinned and fall short of the glory of God, being justified as a gift by His grace through the redemption which is in Christ Jesus.
> —Romans 3:23-24

> Here is a trustworthy saying that deserves full acceptance: Christ Jesus came into the world to save sinners – of who I am the worst.
> —1 Timothy 1:15 NIV

We recognize that we are bondservants of the Lord and choose to die daily to all areas of selfishness, pride, arrogance, self-seeking, self-promotion or anything not rooted and grounded in the love of God.

> I affirm, brethren, by the boasting in you which I have in Christ Jesus our Lord, I die daily.
> —1 Corinthians 15:31

Therefore, since we have so great a cloud of witnesses surrounding us, let us also lay aside every encumbrance and the sin which so easily entangles us, and let us run with endurance the race that is set before us. —Hebrews 12:1

Our heart's purpose is to follow the Father's heart in all we do, in all we say, and in all we pray.

Therefore Jesus answered and was saying to them, "Truly, truly, I say to you, the Son can do nothing of Himself, unless it is something He sees the Father doing; for whatever the Father does, these things the Son also does in like manner." —John 5:19

We rest in the Lord and trust in His ways, leaning into Him in every situation.

Return to your rest, O my soul, for the Lord has dealt bountifully with you. —Psalm 116:7

There is more than enough to do all that the Lord has called us to do. We have no lack.

And let endurance have its perfect result, so that you may be perfect and complete, lacking in nothing.
—James 1:4

So that you are not lacking in any gift, awaiting eagerly the revelation of our Lord Jesus Christ.
—1 Corinthians 1:7

By faith, through the blood of Jesus Christ, we have access to heaven where an abundance of every resource is available when we need it, for God has promised to supply all our needs according to His riches and glory in Christ Jesus.

> And my God will supply all your needs according to His riches in glory in Christ Jesus.
>
> —Philippians 4:19

> I pray that the eyes of your heart may be enlightened, so that you will know what is the hope of His calling, what are the riches of the glory of His inheritance in the saints, and what is the surpassing greatness of His power toward us who believe.
>
> —Ephesians 1:18-19

We release heaven on earth, as Jesus taught us to pray to the Father from our position seated with Christ in heavenly places.

> "Your kingdom come. Your will be done, on earth as it is in heaven." —Matthew 6:10

> Therefore if you have been raised up with Christ, keep seeking the things above, where Christ is, seated at the right hand of God. Set your mind on the things above, not on the things that are on earth. For you have died and your life is hidden with Christ in God. —Colossians 3:1-3

We yield to Holy Spirit daily, to be filled with His life breath, power and fire.

Now may the God of hope fill you with all joy and peace in believing, so that you will abound in hope by the power of the Holy Spirit.   —Romans 15:13

And the disciples were continually filled with joy and with the Holy Spirit.   —Acts 13:52

We have faith in God and believe in the promises of God. We will contend for His bride to come into these promises.

Let perseverance finish its work so that you may be mature and complete, not lacking anything.
—James 1:4 NIV

Let us rejoice and be glad and give the glory to Him, for the marriage of the Lamb has come and His bride has made herself ready.   —Revelation 19:7

We are radical, extravagant worshippers who love to love God!

Let all who seek You rejoice and be glad in You; And let those who love Your salvation say continually, "Let God be magnified."   —Psalm 70:4

So David said to Michal, "It was before the Lord, who chose me above your father and above all his house, to appoint me ruler over the people of the Lord, over

Israel; therefore I will celebrate before the Lord. I will be more lightly esteemed than this and will be humble in my own eyes, but with the maids of whom you have spoken, with them I will be distinguished."

—2 Samuel 6:21-22

We will not allow doubt, unbelief, or negativity to dwell in our hearts.

Truly I say to you, whoever says to this mountain, "Be taken up and cast into the sea," and does not doubt in his heart, but believes that what he says is going to happen, it will be granted him.

—Mark 11:23

Take care, brethren, that there not be in any one of you an evil, unbelieving heart that falls away from the living God.   —Hebrews 3:12

We are called to pour ourselves out from a place of rest, to be a blessing to the body of Christ. This is our joy and our privilege!

Therefore, let us fear if, while a promise remains of entering His rest, any one of you may seem to have come short of it.   —Hebrews 4:1

Therefore encourage one another and build up one another, just as you also are doing.

—1 Thessalonians 5:11

We give thanks in all things and choose to rejoice in the Lord always! We know that God is good and will not believe any other voice that would try to pull us away from the Spirit of Truth.

But when He, the Spirit of truth, comes, He will guide you into all the truth; for He will not speak on His own initiative, but whatever He hears, He will speak; and He will disclose to you what is to come.

—John 16:13

Always giving thanks for all things in the name of our Lord Jesus Christ to God, even the Father; and be subject to one another in the fear of Christ.

—Ephesians 5:20-21

We know that God's glory is His loving-kindness, grace and favor, which He gives us freely.

Now behold, your servant has found favor in your sight, and you have magnified your lovingkindness, which you have shown me by saving my life; but I cannot escape to the mountains, for the disaster will overtake me and I will die.   —Genesis 19:19

He predestined us to adoption as sons through Jesus Christ to Himself, according to the kind intention of His will, to the praise of the glory of His grace, which He freely bestowed on us in the Beloved.

—Ephesians 1:5-6

He is relentless in revealing His truth to us and we are captivated by His gaze, resting in His love.

You will give truth to Jacob and unchanging love to Abraham, which You swore to our forefathers from the days of old. —Micah 7:20

Grace, mercy and peace will be with us, from God the Father and from Jesus Christ, the Son of the Father, in truth and love. —2 John 1:3

We are sealed in the holy fire of God's love, set apart for Him and completely devoted to Him. Nothing can separate us from His love as we abide in Christ Jesus and He abides in us.

But in all these things we overwhelmingly conquer through Him who loved us. For I am convinced that neither death, nor life, nor angels, nor principalities, nor things present, nor things to come, nor powers, nor height, nor depth, nor any other created thing, will be able to separate us from the love of God, which is in Christ Jesus our Lord. —Romans 8:37-39

In Him, you also, after listening to the message of truth, the gospel of your salvation—having also believed, you were sealed in Him with the Holy Spirit of promise, who is given as a pledge of our inheritance, with a view to the redemption of God's own possession, to the praise of His glory.

—Ephesians 1:13-14

In Him we have faith, hope and love, which remain forever and ever.

And now these three remain: faith, hope and love. But the greatest of these is love.

—1 Corinthians 13:13 NIV

We always thank God for all of you and continually mention you in our prayers. We remember before our God and Father your work produced by faith, your labor prompted by love, and your endurance inspired by hope in our Lord Jesus Christ.

—1 Thessalonians 1:2-4 NIV

Conclusion

Transformational Reformers

AS INTERCESSORS we can be transformational reformers, but first we must understand who we are and what we have available to us. We need to agree with the Father and His Kingdom, and this requires revelation and understanding. It's not enough to just read the Word. We must also interact with the living Word. We need the life of the Holy Spirit to infuse us with His dunamis courage and grace to live morally excellent lives that release hope.

Intercession not only changes our lives through what Christ has done for us, but it also changes our world view so that we can transform and bring reformation to bear in our spheres of influence. To reform means that by removing faults, we bring improvement; we eliminate undesirable habits. When we transform, we bring about radical change. We bring light and life into dark situations. When we participate in the process of transformational reformation, we release the Kingdom of God into our God-given spheres of influence.

When we intercede, we are aiming to resolve conflict and to initiate action that will impact someone else's life. We become mediators in a process of arbitration and negotiation. We can also become what Bob Hartley calls "Hope Reformers." Hope reformers bring the mediation of heaven into dark places, standing in the gap as arbitrators of heaven so that the promises of God can be released. They transfer the goodness of our Father God to others, helping them to navigate away from a path of death and destruction to the *only* path of life and light, which is Jesus Christ.

My friend Mary is a Hope Reformer. She lives in hope. She is an encourager who releases hope. She has a testimony of the keeping power of God, reminding those around her to live on Papa God's playground and live in the embrace of child-like faith so as to discover the joy of the One who will defeat every bully that would try to come against His children. She releases hope through her life, her words, her art, and the way she loves God and His children. Mary is a Hope Reformer who lives in the river! We all have the ability to be hope reformers, to jump into the River of Life and release hope through our words, our prayers, our decrees, and our declarations.

In October of 2008 Bob Hartley prophesied over me, unlocking for me a greater understanding of my calling. Here are some excerpts from that word:

And you're going to minister hope to the hearts ... I believe you are to open up the compartment of hope, which is confident expectation for God in the land of the living – to give courage to the heart. So I hear that proclamation and I believe the Lord will give you more orations, proclamations, and don't worry, you'll blast out their demons. You will wear demons out. That's appropriate, you know. If people were just patient a little bit, but people are about to win, wearing their demons out, you know, and have a total breakthrough into a new realm; but they surrender too quickly. So, I believe you are to be a perspective-bringer. And you keep the proclamations. You shout all the louder!

What a revelation! We change and reform by bringing into situations the words of hope from our God. Just imagine what could happen if we really grasp the power of God inside of us to speak life and to wear out the demons around us. I believe the body of Christ would no longer be deformed, but become the strong and courageous deliverers we are meant to be!

Appendix

DURING MY ORDINATION with the Apostolic Network of Global Awakening in 2009, Patricia King gave a word about the Lovelution and the Lovelutionaries God was preparing. Among the many voices in that season who spoke of the Love Revolution, the word Lovelutionary rang true to me. When she prayed for me, she released this word, saying it was for me. Shortly after returning home from this gathering, the Lord gave me this decree. I truly believe it releases what He is doing through our stance of being His holy advocates of love and justice.

Lovelutionaries Arise
by Tracee Anne Loosle

There's a cry from heaven penetrating the earth
The sound of awakening shaking every system
Resonating with the heartbeat of the Father
Lovelutionaries arise with holy justice of heaven

There have been revolutions and revolutionaries
Changing history and dealing with travesties
Today a new breed is coming to birth a Lovelution
Lovelutinaries are arising to set the captives free

There's a new word ringing in the air today
Calling to the ones who have laid down their lives
Lovelutionaries, arise for your hour has come
Love is on your side as you partner with Christ

For One paid the price for all to come freely
His life marks these called to make all things right
They bear the creed "One for all and all for One"
Holy Lovelutionaries filled with the True Love Light

There's a new sound reverberating in these hearts
Rhythm of a holy love war delivering freedom
Love that wars against hatred and prejudice
Lovelutionary power and healing through the Son

In their hearts the Word of God encased in His love
Their weapons of praise binding the enemy's plans
From their mouths prophetic words releasing destiny
Faces like flint, hearts ablaze take back the land

There's a new way being birthed through these ones
Lovelutionaries arise! Deliver His own from sin's plight
A Lovelution stirring the heart and souls of man
Bearing the Kingdom of heaven, love power and might

May intrepid warriors awaken and arise as Lovelutionaries!

Intrepid Warrior Proclamation

WE ARE INTREPID WARRIORS, an overcoming, worshipping warrior bride, called to the Lord's side in the end-time army.

Great grace is poured out upon us as we humble ourselves before the Lord.

We seek the Lord first in all things, and keep our eyes fixed on Him.

As we pursue God's Kingdom and His purposes first, we choose the Lord's will and not our own.

We recognize our need of a Savior and fall upon the Lord Jesus.

We recognize that we are bondservants of the Lord and choose to die daily to all areas of selfishness, pride, arrogance, self-seeking, self-promotion or anything not rooted and grounded in the love of God.

Our heart's purpose is to follow the Father's heart in all we do, in all we say, and in all we pray.

We rest in the Lord and trust in His ways, leaning into Him in every situation.

There is more than enough to do all that the Lord has called us to do. We have no lack.

By faith, through the blood of Jesus Christ, we have access to heaven where an abundance of every resource is available when we need it, for God has promised to supply all our needs according to His riches and glory in Christ Jesus.

We release heaven on earth, as Jesus taught us to pray to the Father from our position seated with Christ in heavenly places.

We yield to Holy Spirit daily, to be filled with His life breath, power and fire.

We have faith in God and believe in the promises of God. We will contend for His bride to come into these promises.

We are radical, extravagant worshippers who love to love God!

We will not allow doubt, unbelief, or negativity to dwell in our hearts.

We are called to pour ourselves out from a place of rest, to be a blessing to the body of Christ. This is our joy and our privilege!

We give thanks in all things and choose to rejoice in the Lord always! We know that God is good and will not believe any other voice that would try to pull us away from the Spirit of Truth.

We know that God's glory is His loving-kindness, grace and favor which He gives us freely.

He is relentless in revealing His truth to us and we are captivated by His gaze, resting in His love.

We are sealed in the holy fire of God's love, set apart for Him and completely devoted to Him. Nothing can separate us from His love as we abide in Christ Jesus and He abides in us.

In Him we have faith, hope and love, which remain forever and ever!

To contact Tracee Anne Loosle, find out more about
her ministry or order more copies of *Intrepid Warriors
- Living a Life of Fearles Intercession*, please visit her
website:

intrepidheart.org

Additional copies of this book and other
book titles from XP Publishing are also available at the
store at XPministries.com

For wholesale orders for bookstores and ministries,
please contact: resource@xpministries.com

This book is also available to bookstores through
anchordistributors.com

XPpublishing.com
XP Ministries